# THE
# TRINITY

D1113341

# THE
# TRINITY

## Philip W. Butin

**Foundations of Christian Faith**
Published by Geneva Press in Conjunction with
the Office of Theology and Worship, Presbyterian Church (U.S.A.)

Scripture quotations from the New Revised Standard Version of the Bible are copyright © 1989 by the Division of Christian Education of the National Council of the Churches of Christ in the U.S.A. and are used by permission.

*Book design by Sharon Adams*
*Cover design by Night & Day Design*

*First edition*
Published by Geneva Press
Louisville, Kentucky

This book is printed on acid-free paper that meets the American National Standards Institute Z39.48 standard. ♾

PRINTED IN THE UNITED STATES OF AMERICA

01 02 03 04 05 06 07 08 09 10 — 10 9 8 7 6 5 4 3 2 1

**Library of Congress Cataloging-in-Publication Data**
Butin, Philip Walker.
    The Trinity / Philip W. Butin.—1st ed.
        p. cm.—(Foundations of Christian faith)
    ISBN 0-664-50140-0 (pbk. : alk. paper)
    1. Trinity.  I. Title.  II. Series.

BT111.2.B885 2000
231'.044—dc21                                        00-034755

### St. Patrick's Breastplate
#### Patrick of Ireland (389–461)

*I bind unto myself the name,*
*the strong name of the Trinity,*
*by invocation of the same,*
*the Three in One, the One in Three,*
*of whom all nature has creation,*
*eternal Father, Spirit, Word.*
*Praise to the Lord of my salvation,*
*salvation is of Christ the Lord. Amen.*

# Contents

# Series Foreword

*T*he books in the Foundations of Christian Faith series explore central elements of Christian belief. These books are intended for persons on the edge of faith as well as for those with strong Christian commitment. The writers are women and men of vital faith and keen intellect who know what it means to be an everyday Christian.

Each of the twelve books in the series focuses on a theme central to the Christian faith. The authors hope to encourage you as you grapple with the big, important issues that accompany our faith in God. Thus, Foundations of Christian Faith includes volumes on the Trinity, what it means to be human, worship and sacraments, Jesus Christ, the Bible, the Holy Spirit, the church, life as a Christian, political and social engagement, religious pluralism, creation and new creation, and dealing with suffering.

You may read one or two of the books that deal with issues you find particularly interesting, or you may wish to read them all in order to gain a deeper understanding of your faith. You may read the books by yourself or together with others. In any event, I trust that you will find a fuller awareness of the living God who is made known in Jesus Christ through the present power of the Holy Spirit. Christian faith is not about the mastery of ideas. It is about encountering the living God. It is my confident hope that this series of books will lead you more deeply into that encounter.

Charles Wiley
Office of Theology and Worship
Presbyterian Church (U.S.A.)

# Acknowledgments

*I* am grateful for all who have made the writing of this book such an unqualified joy. First, to my congregation, Shepherd of the Valley Presbyterian Church, for embracing your pastor's vision that trinitarian theology—clearly articulated for the church—really can inform and guide our unique ministry together. You have patiently put up with study leaves and study days, you have prayed for the fruitfulness of this book in the lives of its readers, you have carefully read and reacted to its many drafts, and you have engaged me in vigorous discussion of why it matters. I am truly indebted. This book is both from and for you.

I also wish to express profound thanks to John Burgess and Charles Wiley of the Office of Theology and Worship of the Presbyterian Church (U.S.A.), originator and editor, respectively, of this remarkable series, whose vision of theology from and for the church corresponds so closely to my own. The other authors in this uniquely collaborative series have greatly improved the book with their wisdom and their careful attention to clear communication. Dr. Geoffrey Wainwright, my theological mentor and friend, graciously read the entire manuscript and offered many valuable suggestions. The Union Theological Seminary Library in Virginia assumed considerable risk in loaning me the books I needed through the mail, for use in New Mexico. The library staff has been exceptionally helpful. My wife, Rev. Jan Butin, and my two children, Matthew and Kristen, have sacrificially offered much patience, support, and prayer in this endeavor.

My prayer is that each person who picks up this book might be apprehended, grasped, and transformed by the knowledge, grace, and love of the one God who is Father, Son, and Holy Spirit. To the extent that this prayer is realized, my purpose in writing will be fulfilled.

*Albuquerque, New Mexico*
*Trinity 1999*

# Introduction

*C*hristian faith is rooted in the historic conviction that the one, unique God is triune, existing as Father, Son, and Holy Spirit. "Triune" is a compound adjective that points to the historic but mysterious Christian conviction that God is both three and one.

Why believe in this God? Why not formulate some other way of thinking about God that makes more sense? A way that offends fewer sensibilities? A way that risks fewer misunderstandings? Why not think of God in simpler, cleaner, less controversial terms?

The answer is that Christian faith stands or falls with "the strong name of the Trinity." Christian teaching about the Trinity is the heart and center of Christian faith. It is only if God is triune that we can be sure that God can be and wants to be known by us. It is only if God is triune that we can know that God is gracious toward us. In the Trinity is our confidence that "God is unalterably oriented toward us in love."[1] Christian belief in the Trinity encapsulates the good news. In spite of our failings, our self-centeredness, our stubbornness, and the hurt we cause ourselves and others, God has entered our world and poured out the divine love for us once for all in Jesus Christ. This same God condescends to live within and among us as the Holy Spirit, gently reconnecting us to God and restoring in us the strength,

---

[1]Catherine Mowry LaCugna, *God for Us: The Trinity and Christian Life* (San Francisco: HarperSanFrancisco, 1991), 245.

goodness, and purpose that only God can offer. That is why ordinary, everyday Christians have at least as much stake in the trinitarian character of our faith as do academic scholars. This is not something that can be left to the "experts." Trinitarian faith belongs to the church. It is *our* faith. It is the faith of our baptism.

1

# Baptized in the Strong Name

*Philip Walker Butin, I baptize you in the name of the
Father, and of the Son, and of the Holy Spirit.*

*I* don't remember hearing these words at my baptism. Still,
I know the minister pronounced them as the water was
poured three times over my tiny, bald head. These words
announced to my parents and the assembled congregation
the identity of the God in whose name this rambunctious
baby was being baptized. One baptism in which the water
was poured three times. One divine name which is also
mysteriously threefold: Father, Son, and Holy Spirit—the
strong name of the Trinity.

The words spoken at our baptism are deeply traditional.
They bear within themselves the vast legacy of Christian
worship, belief, and practice that connects the church of the
New Testament and the church of our own baptism. Yet
these words are startlingly contemporary each time they are
spoken in the baptismal celebration of a Christian congregation. They sound out freshly and uniquely each time a
specific human name is linked with the mysteriously threefold divine name.

Whether or not we remember these words, those who are
baptized know that they were spoken by the pastor in our
own baptism. Over the years, they have been reinforced and
internalized as we have heard them articulated again and
again in the worship of our congregation. We have reaffirmed them repeatedly ourselves as we have promised "to
guide and nurture . . . by word and deed, with love and
prayer" others who are baptized: our own children, nieces

and nephews, and children and adults within various congregations to which we have belonged as members of the one church of Jesus Christ. You may have come to question the meaning of your baptism. We can grow calloused to the joy and possibility of an act of worship that has come to feel perfunctory or routine. You may have become justifiably disillusioned with the minister, or the church, or the entire faith tradition connected with your original baptism. You may feel profoundly skeptical about whether your original, unremembered baptism made any difference at all in your life. Some people raised in the church have even gone so far as to be rebaptized in another faith tradition after a particularly important experience of personal faith.

But to forget our own baptism would be to forget who we are. "Remembrance" in biblical tradition is vastly deeper and broader than conscious awareness of individual personal experience. As the Hebrews of Josiah's time (621 B.C.) heard the words of the rediscovered "book of the law" read out loud in worship (2 Kings 22:8–23:3), centuries stood between them and the ancestors whom their God had earlier liberated from the bondage of Egypt (Exodus 12–13). Yet in remembrance, the events of the past became mysteriously contemporary and transforming:

> When your children ask you in time to come, "What is the meaning of the decrees and the statutes and the ordinances that Yahweh our God has commanded you?" then you shall say to your children, "*We* were Pharaoh's slaves in Egypt, but Yahweh brought *us* out of Egypt with a mighty hand. Yahweh displayed *before our eyes* great and awesome signs and wonders against Egypt, against Pharoah and all his household. He brought *us* out from there in order to bring *us* in, to give *us* the land that he promised on oath to our ancestors. (Deut. 6:20–23; emphasis mine)

This same profound sense of "remembrance" applies to our baptism. Its meaning and power are not frustrated by the limitations of our human memory, our experience, our relationships, our denominational associations, or even our faith. *The name into which we are baptized is "the strong name of the Trinity."* The divine reality which that name identifies holds each of us, as baptized believers, firmly and securely in the divine embrace, keeping covenant and steadfast love to the thousandth generation.

Through the trinitarian words of our baptism, the triune God sets forth and bestows our very identity. They are performative words. When a woman and a man stand before each other in a public ceremony and promise, "Before God and these witnesses, I take you to be my husband/wife," they become what they promise. Through the couple's wedding vows, God constitutes the covenant relationship of marriage. In the same way, through the words "Philip Walker Butin, I baptize you in the name of the Father, and of the Son, and of the Holy Spirit," God actually claimed me and made me God's own precious child.

The words of our baptism are also dynamic words, whose power is dramatically enacted in symbolic liturgical actions. First, water is poured. Next, we are touched three times with the cleansing and refreshing wetness that sacramentally enacts God's claim on our lives. Finally, we are immersed in the prayers, love, and nurture of our own Christian congregation—its worship, its ministry, and its faith.

The words of our baptism speak volumes about each of us, individually and specifically. But they do this by speaking first, and primarily, of the triune God to whom we belong.

The words of my baptism tell me *who* I am by telling me *Whose* I am.

## Who God Is, Who We Are

*God said to Moses: "I am who I am."*

God's existence and identity are neither defined by nor dependent upon anything outside of God. Scripture tells us that Yahweh[1] spoke the cryptic words of Exodus 3:14 in response to

---

[1] In Hebrew, this word consists simply of the four consonants יהוה. Thought to have been pronounced "Yahweh," it is the proper name for God in Exodus and throughout the Old Testament. Exodus 3:13–16 suggests that it is derived from Yahweh's mysterious statement, "I am who I am," to Moses. It was regarded as too holy to pronounce in the Hebrew reading of the scriptures. Instead, the Hebrew word for *Lord* (אדני, *adonai*) was substituted.

## 4    The Trinity

Moses' question, "If I come to the Israelites and say to them, 'The God of your ancestors has sent me to you,' and they ask me, 'What is his name?' what shall I say to them?"_ _I am who I am._ Is it a name? Or is it the refusal to be limited or controlled by a name? Perhaps both. It simultaneously reveals and conceals. If Yahweh had not willed to be known, the burning bush incident would never have occurred. Yet the identity revealed there is utterly beyond all human comprehension. Still, here and throughout the Old Testament, the name "Yahweh" is recognized as God's self-identification. Yahweh is the specific God known in the biblical stories of Abraham and Sarah, Miriam, Moses, Zipporah, Rahab, Mary, Paul, Priscilla, John, and indeed all of God's people. Yahweh's identity is established, revealed, and declared in divine words, commitments, and acts. Who God is becomes known in what Yahweh brings to pass. Yahweh is the One who is always faithful to the divine promise.[2]

It is *this* God whose mysterious identity is the basis of our identity.

### Jesus' Baptism, Our Baptism

*Now when all the people were baptized, and when Jesus also had been baptized and was praying, the heaven was opened, and the Holy Spirit descended upon him in bodily form like a dove. And a voice came from heaven, "You are my Son, the Beloved; with you I am well pleased."*

Luke 3:21–22

The early Christians were confident that the same God who spoke to Moses at the burning bush also spoke at Jesus' baptism, identifying the humble son of Mary as the "son of Yahweh," and as the "servant of Yahweh" toward whom the Old Testament hope is directed. The words spoken by Yahweh to Jesus at his baptism are drawn precisely from Old Testament passages that articulate that hope. In Psalm 2 we find a classic expression of Israel's messianic expectation of a royal successor who would embody the

---

[2] Cf. Robert Jenson, *The Triune Identity: God According to the Gospel* (Philadelphia: Fortress Press, 1982), 40.

fulfillment of Yahweh's promises to David's offspring. In verse 7, Yahweh says to the awaited Messiah, the anointed royal heir: "You are my son; (today) I have begotten you." The first "Servant Song" in the book of Isaiah begins in chapter 42, where Israel's hope for the anointed "servant of Yahweh" who is chosen to deliver them comes into clear focus:

> Here is my servant, whom I uphold,
>   my chosen, in whom my soul delights;
> I have put my spirit upon him;
>   he will bring forth justice to the nations.
> (Isa. 42:1)

When Yahweh says to Jesus, "You are my Son, the Beloved; with you I am well pleased," the gospels are presenting Jesus as the Messiah, the focus of Israel's hope. The moment of Jesus' baptism anticipates and prefigures the later and fuller revelation of his messianic identity that will occur throughout his life, ministry, suffering, death, resurrection, ascension, and the pouring out of the Holy Spirit at Pentecost. The familiar word "Christ" is the Greek translation for the Hebrew word *mashiach*, which means, "messiah" or "anointed one." In Jesus' baptism, Yahweh claims and identifies Jesus as Messiah and divine Son, through the anointing of the Holy Spirit.

The gospel of Matthew was written within first-century Jewish communities that had come to faith in Jesus as Messiah. These were communities who prayed daily, "Hear, O Israel, the Lord your God, the Lord is one." They were deeply committed to the traditional Jewish conviction of God's utter simplicity, God's oneness. This highlights a remarkable fact. This same gospel concludes with Jesus' command that his disciples throughout the world be baptized into a fuller, threefold revelation of the divine name. In this revelation, the divine identity of Yahweh is intrinsically connected with God's self-identification in Jesus the Messiah, the one who was uniquely anointed with the Holy Spirit:

> "All authority in heaven and on earth has been given to me. Go therefore and make disciples of all nations, baptizing them in the name of the Father and of the Son and of the Holy Spirit, and teaching them to obey everything that I have commanded

you. And remember, I am with you always, to the end of the age." (Matt. 28:18–20)

The word "name" is singular. Yet that name here is also mysteriously threefold. Thus Christians, followers of the Messiah, recognize and name Yahweh—the great "I AM," who revealed the divine identity to Moses at the burning bush—in the New Testament revelation of the God into whose threefold name we are baptized. Together with the earliest believers, we realize today through both the event and the living out of our own baptisms that Jesus was the Son of God. We realize that Yahweh is the One whom Jesus called "Father." We realize that the Holy Spirit is the bond of Jesus' connection to Yahweh and the source of empowerment for his mission of announcing and inaugurating God's reign on earth.

### Identity in Relatedness

*There is one body and one Spirit,*
*just as you were called to the one hope of your calling,*
*one Lord, one faith, one baptism,*
*one God and Father of all, who is above all and through*
*all and in all.*

Ephesians 4:4–6

Christian baptism is certainly individual and personal, both in its administration and in its meaning. But each individual is baptized into the reality of the church, the community of God's people. In this common baptism, our personal identity lies in our relatedness. Primarily, we are related to the triune God. But because God's own identity lies in the threefold relatedness of Father, Son, and Holy Spirit, our personal identity lies no less crucially in our relatedness to one another.

The identity-in-relatedness that we receive in our baptism threatens and subverts cultural values that obscure the communal vision of God's reign. A common saying of Jesus' time was, "I thank God that I was not born a Gentile, a slave, or a woman." In that climate, the apostle Paul declared boldly,

As many of you as were baptized into Christ have clothed yourselves with Christ. There is no longer Jew or Greek, there is no longer slave or free, there is no longer male and female; for all of you are one in Christ Jesus. And if you belong to Christ, then you are Abraham's offspring, heirs according to the promise. (Gal. 3:27–29)

A few verses later, Paul continues in explicitly trinitarian baptismal language:

When the fullness of time had come, God sent his Son, born of a woman, born under the law, in order to redeem those who were under the law, so that we might receive adoption as God's sons and daughters. And because you are God's own sons and daughters, God has sent the Spirit of his Son into our hearts, crying, 'Abba! Father!' So you are no longer a slave but a son or daughter, and if a son or daughter, then also an heir, through God. (Gal. 4:4–7, author's translation)

Just as God's identity is in God's own triune relatedness, our identity is found in the baptismal community: the extended, loving family that we have always hoped for but only rarely experienced; the place of mutuality that too many of us know only through our unfulfilled longings; the home where we belong; the lap in which we discover *Whose*—and therefore also *who*— we are.

## We Belong to This God

*Pues si vivimos para Él vivimos,*
*y si morimos para Él morimos.*
*Sea que vivamos o que*
  *muramos*
*Somos del Señor, somos*
  *del Señor.*[3]

If we live, we live for God.
And if we die, we die for God.
Regardless of whether we live
  or die,
we belong to God. We belong
  to God.

---

[3] See *The Presbyterian Hymnal* (Louisville, Ky.: Westminster/John Knox Press, 1990), hymn 400. The English translation is my own.

This popular contemporary Hispanic hymn expresses the Christian confidence—rooted in Romans 14:8 and 1 Corinthians 6:19–20—that we belong to God. Our baptism in the threefold divine name is the basis of that confidence. The hymn reflects a prominent theme of the sixteenth-century Heidelberg Catechism, written to communicate Christian faith to children. The teacher asked, "What is your only comfort, in life and in death?" The children responded, "That I belong, body and soul, in life and in death, not to myself, but to my faithful savior Jesus Christ."[4]

Echoes of this same tradition are evident in a recent (1990) and more explicitly trinitarian Christian statement of faith:

> In life and in death, we belong to God,
> Through the grace of our Lord Jesus Christ,
> the love of God,
> and the communion of the Holy Spirit.
> We believe in the one triune God,
> the Holy One of Israel,
> whom alone we worship and serve.[5]

These ringing affirmations of Christian confidence are rooted in the Christian experience of baptism in the triune name.

### Not Just Any God

*God is not truly known,*
*unless our faith distinctly conceives three persons in one*
    *essence;*
*and from this the efficacy and fruit of baptism flow:*
*God the Father adopts us in his Son,*
*and through the Spirit reforms us into righteousness.*
                                            John Calvin, 1555[6]

---

[4] *The Constitution of the Presbyterian Church (U.S.A.),* Part I: *Book of Confessions* (Louisville, Ky.: Office of the General Assembly, 1999), 3.1.

[5] Ibid., 10.1.

[6] *Harmony of the Evangelists, Vol. III (Calvin's New Testament Commentaries),* ed. David and Thomas Torrance (Edinburgh: T. & T. Clark, 1972), on Matthew 28:19.

The God of our baptism is not just any God. God is certainly not cosmic Play-Doh that we can mold to our liking. It is dangerous to think we can describe God in whatever set of words suits us. The content of the biblical story of Yahweh's relationship with Israel and Yahweh's self-revelation in Jesus Christ—the One anointed by the Holy Spirit—defines for us both who God is, and what God is not. There has always been a powerful human temptation to project or construct a god on whom to focus our worship, a god who reflects our own preferences and who mirrors and legitimates the values of our culture.

John Calvin was one of the most influential Christian reformers of the sixteenth century. He was acutely concerned about the human temptation to worship gods of our own creation. Without hesitation he called this temptation idolatry. He regarded God's triune nature as "a special mark to distinguish himself more precisely from idols." In idolatry, we project or construct a god on the basis of human needs, desires, or ideas. In the Trinity, *God the Father reveals God's own self to us in the Son, by the Holy Spirit.* When we make idols, we worship what we have created. When we direct our faith to the triune God we worship the One by whom, through whom, and in whom we are created. Calvin recognized that in the New Testament, baptism in the name of the Father, and of the Son, and of the Holy Spirit was what sacramentally enacted the connection of believers with the one God of biblical faith, Creator of heaven and earth.[7]

The temptation to idolatry is subtle. It affects us all. Recent philosophical reflection on language has emphasized just how much our grasp of the realities we attempt to conceptualize—and even the realities we perceive—is shaped by the particular words we choose with which to refer to them. This awareness cuts two ways.

First, as cultural sensitivity to the historic oppression of women increases, questions are rightly being asked about whether traditional trinitarian terms for God (especially the term

---

[7] John Calvin, *Institutes of the Christian Religion (1559)*, ed. J. T. McNeill (Philadelphia: Westminster Press, 1960), 1.13.2, 16.

"Father") might not inevitably reinforce traditionally harmful sexist stereotypes about God's relationship to women, and about women's place in a traditionally male-dominated church and world. For many, this question has already been settled in the affirmative. The last twenty years have witnessed an unprecedented movement to remove all language for God rooted in male imagery from Christian worship, hymns, and even scripture.

Mainstream Christian theology has never argued that God is male. But our language has been such that this impression is often communicated. Indeed, a whole culture within the Christian community seems to suggest or assume that maleness is to be equated with divinity, and that therefore femaleness is second-best or even antithetical to divinity.

God is the sovereign Creator. Gender is an attribute of the creation. The Creator of gender is not subject to it. Growing public awareness of this historic Christian conviction, combined with deepened cultural sensitivity to the broader issues of gender and sexism, have understandably led many to eliminate the use of male pronouns when referring to God.  In addition, following biblical usage, many now regard it as important to supplement the use of male images in referring to God with female and feminine images consistent with scripture wherever possible, in order to constantly correct misunderstandings of Christian tradition and to continually expand our imaginative resources for receiving God's self-revelation. Concern for the elimination of oppressive patriarchal structures, and patterns of thought and speech that may reinforce these structures, is something that a wide variety of spiritually sensitive, thinking Christians can gladly share.

However, where trinitarian language is concerned, the issues become quite complex, and the stakes become incomparably higher. How do we improve upon the language for God that scripture attributes to Jesus himself? Over time, what would be the consequences of abandoning the language reaffirmed by the Christian community across two millennia in the formative worship event in which—by the Holy Spirit—the God we know in Jesus Christ becomes ours: the language of the classic Christian baptismal formula? From what standpoint could we possibly determine whether an alternative formulation would carry the same weight of meaning and tradition that has historically been carried by the strong name of the Trinity?

In asking these questions, we have already touched on our second point. It is a mirror image of the point about the power of language. We need to be consistent in our analysis of the powerful role of language in shaping our construals and even our perceptions of reality. If we are, this analysis will give us pause in too easily altering the crucial language formulas that have shaped our apprehension of the God of the biblical story throughout Christian history.

In the justified concern to find a solution to the genuine problem of how we can speak of God in language that does not reinforce patriarchal traditions, we lose more than we gain if the theological convictions that the doctrine of the Trinity was originally developed to express and safeguard are compromised. The greatest danger is that in sacrificing the language of its scripture and its traditions, the church will find itself adrift, with its theology and its worship no longer anchored in the self-revelation of the gracious, triune God of the biblical story who is its source, its reason, and its goal. The crucial question is whether the time-tested meanings invested in the traditional terms can be adequately carried by other words. Asked the other way around, can the church keep continuity with the God revealed in the biblical story if it abandons the traditional, gendered trinitarian terms given to us there? The terms *Father, Son,* and *Holy Spirit* hand over to successive generations the depth of thousands of years of theological discussion, clarification, and development across a huge variety of philosophical, cultural, and linguistic circumstances. If they are lost, how many generations would it take before the church lost touch with the God to whom they refer?

There is a widespread and perhaps unprecedented ecumenical consensus in established theological circles today that the doctrine of the Trinity is at the center of Christian theology. A wide variety of theologians sensitive to gender issues now suggest that the historic trinitarian faith is precisely where Christians should look for intrinsically Christian ways of encouraging and developing new, more egalitarian and participatory relationships and structures throughout society; especially those concerning gender, race, culture, and class. In continuity with this suggestion, one important concern of this book will be to explore how an intrinsically trinitarian apprehension of God—that remains rooted in traditional trinitarian terminology even as it remains open in principle to other possible formulations—can enable us to overcome the negative legacy of patriarchy.

It has always been possible to worship anyone or anything. The brilliant nineteenth-century German philosopher Ludwig Feuerbach rejected the Christianity of his time, because he was convinced that the God his age was worshiping was a mere projection of human desires.[8] Whenever we substitute some other object of our own preference for the worship of the triune God, we are succumbing to an age-old temptation, rather than being "contemporary" or "making God more relevant." Our worship degenerates into a mere diversion unless it is directed to the true and living God: the One Who Is.

The biblical witness testifies that this One is Yahweh. The One Jesus called "Father." The One who called Jesus "my Son, the Beloved." The One whose Spirit descended upon Jesus in the form of a dove at his baptism. In *our* baptism "in the name of the Father and of the Son and of the Holy Spirit," we have God's own assurance that the One we worship—the One to whom we belong—is this same triune God, the Holy One of Israel. It is this God alone whom we must worship and serve.

---

[8] See Ludwig Feuerbach, *The Essence of Christianity*, trans. George Eliot (New York: Harper & Row, 1957).

# 2

# Recognizing God as Triune

*I*n the radiant light of Jesus' resurrection and the Holy Spirit's outpouring at the festival of Pentecost, his early followers found themselves constrained to speak about both who God is and what God does in terms that we would now call "trinitarian." The Holy Spirit gave them the confidence that in Jesus Christ, they had seen and heard and touched Yahweh, the God of Israel.[1] Their hearts burned with the conviction that Jesus—the One who had been conceived by the Holy Spirit—was "Emmanuel," a Hebrew phrase that means "God with us."[2]

In the New Testament, the doctrine of the Trinity is not yet spelled out as church councils would later define it. Trinitarian language and awareness emerged gradually and spontaneously, as early believers sought to articulate the divine glory they beheld in Jesus, and to describe and claim the life-transforming presence and power of God that they experienced through the Holy Spirit. As we have seen already in chapter 1, the practice of trinitarian baptism is one of the earliest expressions of this growing awareness. First Peter is thought by some to be a sermon preached to a group of early Christians in connection with their baptism. It begins with the trinitarian claim that Christians are those "who have been chosen and destined by God the Father and sanctified by the Spirit to be obedient to Jesus Christ and to be sprinkled with his blood" (1:2).

---

[1] Cf. 1 John 1:1–7.
[2] Matthew 1:23.

This is where the path toward the full recognition of God's triunity begins. In the New Testament and the early church, baptized followers of Jesus struggled for adequate terminology to express their growing awareness that Father, Son, and Spirit are each genuinely divine and also intimately united with one another, both in God's own divine reality and in God's work in human lives and in the world.

### New Testament Sources of Trinitarian Faith

> *Through [Christ] both of us [Jews and Gentiles] have access in one Spirit to the Father.*
>
> Ephesians 2:18

In the Old Testament and in emerging Judaism, God was sometimes addressed as "Father." The image of God as a tender mother is also reflected in the Hebrew scriptures and continues to serve as a helpful corrective to the misunderstanding that calling God "Father" means God is male.[3] But in response to Jesus' own intimate relationship with God and to his teaching about God, the term *Father* became the characteristic Christian way of talking about and addressing Yahweh, the God of Israel. The New Testament indicates that Jesus regarded and related to Yahweh as his Father in a unique sense that "claimed and defined his entire identity."[4] At Jesus' encouragement, the early Christians freely addressed God as "our Father," since by the Spirit and baptism they were united through faith to Yahweh's unique Son.[5] Often they used the same intimate Aramaic family term ("Abba") that Jesus himself had used,[6] confident that in union with Christ, they too were God's own daughters and sons.

---

[3] Psalm 131, Isaiah 49:15–16, 66:13.

[4] Mary Ann Fatula, *The Triune God of Christian Faith* (Collegeville, Minn.: Liturgical Press, 1990), 27. Cf. Matt. 11:25–27; John 11:41, 12:27–28, 17:1ff.; Col. 1:3; Eph. 1:3; 1 Peter 1:3.

[5] Matt. 6:9; 1 Peter 1:17; John 20:17; 2 Thess. 1:2; 2:16; Rom. 1:7.

[6] Mark 14:36; Gal. 4:6; Rom. 8:15.

Because of his intimate and defining relationship with God his heavenly Father, Jesus was the unique "Son of God."[7] The disciples' recognition of Jesus' unique divine sonship was also rooted in the Old Testament expectation of the coming Messiah.[8] The Gospels of Matthew, Mark, and Luke speak of Jesus taking Peter, John, and James "up a high mountain apart." Jesus is transfigured before them, and in the presence of Moses and Elijah, the divine voice identifies Jesus to them: "This is my Son, the Beloved" (Mark 9:2–8). As Jesus' divine identity became clearer to them after the resurrection, the early Christians openly worshiped[9] and even prayed to this risen Son of God as *Lord*.[10] They did this in direct defiance of Roman laws requiring sole allegiance to the emperor as Lord, and in direct continuity with their normal terminology for Yahweh. Given their uncompromised Jewish conviction of God's oneness, all of this—and especially the number of times Jesus is overtly identified as *God* or as divine—is nothing short of astounding.[11]

The Gospel of John is especially reflective of the early Christian conviction that the eternal God—Yahweh, the Holy One of Israel—is uniquely present and made known in Jesus Christ. The breathtaking prologue (John 1:1–19) focuses all the longings of the major traditions of Greek philosophy on Jesus, with its cosmic claim: "In the beginning was the Word, and the Word was with God, and the Word was God." Verse 11 announces that the same Word "became flesh and made his dwelling place among us, full of grace and truth." Although "no one has ever seen God," "it is God the only Son, who is close to the Father's heart, who has made him fully known" (v. 18). Throughout the rest of John's Gospel, Jesus' persistent use of the phrase "I am" (the precise phrase found in the Greek translation of Ex. 3:13–15 where the divine name is revealed) is a direct claim of his divinity. There are

---

[7] Mark 1:11; 15:39; Acts 9:20.
[8] Ps. 2:7; 2 Sam. 7:10ff.
[9] Phil. 2:9–11.
[10] 1 Cor. 16:22; Rev. 22:20.
[11] 2 Cor. 5:19; Rom. 9:5; Phil. 2:6; Col. 1:15–20; 2:9; Heb. 1:1–14; Titus 2:13; 2 Peter 1:1.

seven instances of this phrase with a variety of predicates,[12] by means of which Jesus reassures his followers that all their needs are met in him. But still more significant are the multiple instances of the phrase in the absolute (with no predicate), in which the mysterious divine name occurs on Jesus' lips directly and without remainder.[13] In John 10:30, Jesus' assertion of his own deity is clear in the claim, "The Father and I are one." Chapter 14 concentrates these claims with the phrases "if you had known me, you would have known my Father also" (v. 7), "whoever has seen me has seen the Father" (v. 9), and "I am in the Father and the Father is in me" (v. 10). After Jesus' resurrection, the Gospel climaxes with the skeptical Thomas's unrestrained confession, "My Lord and my God!" (20:28).

Not only did the early Christians confess God as Father and Jesus as Messiah, Lord, and God, they also spoke of the Holy Spirit as both Lord[14] and God.[15] In both Hebrew and Greek, the words translated "Spirit" are also the primary terms in those languages for "breath" and "wind." Thus, the Spirit of God is God at work in the world: moving, enlivening, influencing, refreshing, and renewing. In the Old Testament, the Spirit of God is associated closely with creation,[16] God's presence,[17] divine guidance,[18] divine inspiration[19] and human life and creativity.[20] In the New Testament, the Holy Spirit is God present and operating with power in the Christian community, in the lives of Christian individuals, and in the world, for the accomplishment and fulfillment of God's purpose. In the Gospels—especially Matthew and Luke—Jesus is conceived, anointed, and sent forth in the Spirit to

---

[12] "I am the bread of life" (6:35), "I am the light of the world" (8:12), "I am the gate" (10:7), "I am the Good Shepherd" (10:11, 14), "I am the resurrection and the life" (11:25), "I am the way, the truth, and the life" (14:6), "I am the vine" (15:1, 5).

[13] John 6:20; 8:23–28, 58; 18:5, 8; cf. Mark 14:62.

[14] 2 Cor. 3:17–18.

[15] Acts 5:3–4.

[16] Gen. 1:2; Ps. 33:6; 104:29–30; Job 33:4; 34:14–15.

[17] Ps. 51:10–11; 139:7.

[18] Ps. 143:10; Isa. 11:2.

[19] Num. 11:25–30, Judg. 3:10; 6:34; 11:29; 15:14; etc.; Isa. 61:1–4.

[20] Gen. 2:7; Ex. 31:1ff.; Job 33:4.

announce and inaugurate the reign of God.[21] In John, the Spirit is intimately associated with both the Father and the Son, and is promised as the "other Advocate (or Helper)" who will be God's presence with the disciples once Christ has gone to the Father.[22] In Acts, the Spirit is associated with the surprising, miracle-working power of God, motivating and moving the church in its evangelistic mission to the world.[23] Paul's writings emphasize the Spirit as the source of faith in Jesus Christ,[24] as the bond of unity between Christians,[25] as the source of the spiritual gifts that equip the church for ministry as Christ's body,[26] as the freeing power of God's transforming grace,[27] as the life and power of God empowering the believer for righteous living,[28] as the pledge or guarantee of Christians' eternal inheritance,[29] and as the source of Christian hope.[30]

In addition to Jesus' baptismal commission according to Matthew 28:18–20, a significant number of Gospel and Pauline texts not only closely correlate the divine work of Father, Son, and Holy Spirit,[31] but also link the three together in ways that anticipate the later and fuller development of Trinitarian doctrine in the early church.[32] Particularly in the Gospel of John and the letter to the Ephesians, the unity of Father, Son, and Spirit in all

---

[21] Cf. Matt. 1:18, 20; Luke 1:35; 4:16–21.

[22] John 14:25–26; 15:26; 16:13–15; 20:22.

[23] Cf. Acts 1:8.

[24] 1 Cor. 12:3; cf. 1 John 4:1–2.

[25] 1 Cor. 12:13.

[26] 1 Cor. 12:4–11.

[27] 2 Cor. 3:17–19.

[28] Rom. 8:1–11; Gal. 5:22–25.

[29] Eph. 1:13–14; 2 Cor. 1:22.

[30] Rom. 15:13.

[31] There are numerous triadic patterns that show the united interaction of Father, Son, and Spirit at key narrative turning points of the Gospels and Acts, including the infancy narratives (Matt. 1:18–25; Luke 1:30–35), the narratives of Jesus' baptism (Mark 1:9–11, Matt. 3:13–17; Luke 3:21–22; John 1:29–34), the longer temptation accounts (Matt. 4:1–11; Luke 4:1–13), Jesus' encounter with Nicodemus (John 3:1–21), and the accounts of the ascension (Acts 1:1–6) and of Pentecost (Acts 2:33–39). For Pauline writings, see especially Gal. 3:11–14; 4:6; 1 Cor. 2:7–13; 2 Cor. 1:21–22; 3:3; 3:17–4:7; Rom. 14:17–18; 15:16, 30; Phil. 3:3; Col. 1:6–8; Eph. 1:3–22; 2:17–22; 3:2–6, 14–19.

[32] 2 Thess. 2:13–14, 1 Cor. 12:4–6; 2 Cor. 13:13; Rom. 1:1–4; Eph. 4:4–6; Titus 3:4–6.

God's work is constantly emphasized.[33] Other New Testament authors also reflect the same awareness.[34]

## Emerging Awareness of God's Triunity

In order to appreciate why God's triunity matters today, it is important to know what is at stake in this historic conviction, and something of how and why Christian belief in the Trinity has developed over the nearly two thousand years since the New Testament. This requires considering some of the crucial contributions to trinitarian belief that Christian teachers and theologians have suggested—and which the church has either embraced or rejected as inadequate—across the church's history. The rest of this chapter will trace the articulation of trinitarian faith through the definitive formulations of the Nicene (A.D. 325) and Constantinopolitan (A.D. 381) Creeds. Chapters 3 and 4 will outline pivotal developments in the doctrine of the Trinity from the fourth century through the present.

## The Clarification of Trinitarian Faith in the Early Church

> *The Church, though dispersed throughout the whole world, even to the ends of the earth, has received from the apostles and their disciples this faith: in one God, the Father Almighty, Maker of heaven, and earth, and the sea, and all things that are in them; and in one Christ Jesus, the Son of God, who became incarnate for our salvation; and in the Holy Spirit.*
>
> Irenaeus, c. 190[35]

Summaries of Christian faith for teaching those seeking baptism became common in the second century. From at least the

---

[33] See especially John 14–17 and Ephesians 1–4.

[34] Heb. 6:4; 10:29; Jude 20, 21; 1 Peter 4:14.

[35] An early summary of Christian belief from *Against Heresies* 1.10.1. See John Leith, ed., *Creeds of the Churches*, 3rd ed. (Louisville, Ky.: John Knox Press, 1982), 21.

year 150 and likely much earlier, they show a characteristically trinitarian shape, confessing faith in the Father, Son, and Holy Spirit of the baptismal formula, and then going on to spell out crucial faith convictions connected with each. Closely related summaries of Christian faith, called "rules of faith," were used in the sacrament of baptism itself, in a question and answer format designed to clarify the threefold identity and the saving work of the God into whom the candidates were being baptized. The Apostles' Creed that ecumenical Christians in the West still say together in worship, and especially at baptism, is a later version of these early baptismal creeds. Through these authoritative triadic summaries of the gospel story, baptized Christians of all social classes, educational levels, and nationalities learned to place their faith in God the Father, in Jesus Christ, and in the Holy Spirit.

The early church was often obliged to clarify what it did believe and confess about God by contrast with what it did not believe. Some expressions of Christian faith proved unable to do justice to the early church's encounter with God in Christ through the Spirit, as passed down in the original New Testament writings. Others were judged inadequate by their consequences for current Christian faith, worship, and practice. As Christian leaders and writers did their best to articulate the church's convictions as to who God is and what God does, turns of thought were sometimes taken that eventually proved—upon deeper reflection—to lead away from instead of toward the path to stable, secure, enduring Christian faith. Over time, efforts to express Christian beliefs that obscured rather than clarifying the truth of God as revealed in Jesus Christ by the Holy Spirit were rejected. These inadequate, unfruitful, counterproductive articulations of faith, which were eventually judged to be dead-end streets, were called *heresies*.

Christian reaffirmation of the oneness of God had already been emphatic in the New Testament.[36] It was clarified in response to

---

[36] Mark 10:18; 12:29; 1 Cor. 8:6; 1 Timothy 1:17; Jude 25; etc.

early speculation that perhaps the Old Testament reflected a judgmental Creator God of law who was fundamentally different from the gracious Redeemer God of the New Testament. This position had been championed by a leader named Marcion, who founded a breakaway church in the middle of the second century. The need to ward off this twisting of the Christian message confirmed orthodox Christians in the confidence that the one God who created all things must be the same God who extends salvation to humankind through Christ, by means of the Holy Spirit.

Another popular second-century spirituality has been designated by historians as *Gnosticism*. Often combined with Christian teachings, Gnosticism emphasized the idea that salvation came through human enlightenment involving special, esoteric knowledge for a privileged few; knowledge that gradually liberated them from the evil material world. Christian conviction that Jesus was the divine Word of God become flesh—God definitively revealed for our salvation in the good divine created world—deepened in response to this religious perspective.

Second-century Christian thinkers defended the young faith against such misunderstandings, and sought to make the orthodox faith understandable to seekers in the surrounding culture. As they did, the simultaneously held convictions that God is one and that God's revelation and work in the world are accomplished by the threefold divine reality of Father, Son, and Holy Spirit emerged hand in hand. These three are distinct, and yet only one God.

A very important early effort to hold these ideas together was made by a lawyer-turned-theologian named Tertullian. Tertullian reacted in North Africa against another heresy, that of Praxeas and his followers. This group blurred the distinction between the Father, Son, and Spirit in a misguided effort to maintain God's unity. In response, Tertullian focused on articulating the unity in distinction within the Trinity, in terms that were to give trinitarian faith its enduring Western and Latin vocabulary. In the Greek language, the term *trias* ("trinity") had already been introduced into Christian discussion of God by Theophilus, bishop of Antioch, about 180. But Tertullian is the first known to use the Latin word *Trinitas* as a direct title for God. In the early 200s, he spoke repeatedly of the Trinity in the absolute, and referred to "the trinity of one divinity: Father, Son, and Holy Spirit."[37] In his efforts to refute Praxeas, he argued that there is a real distinction—but no division—between three divine *persons*, appealing to a single divine *substance* as the basis of God's oneness. "The Father is God, and the Son is God, and the Holy Ghost is God, and each is God"; yet in such a way that there is "one unique substance in three coherent and inseparable Persons." In order to illustrate this unity in distinction, Tertullian appealed to threefold natural analogies such as a root, a tree, and its fruit; the sun, its rays, and the ray's apex; or a water source, the river which flows from it, and the tributary which emerges from the river. He did not believe these analogies fully indicated God's trinitarian nature, nor did he propose them as alternative ways to say "Father, Son, and Holy Spirit." He intended them only as illustrations of how distinction and inseparable unity can coexist in the same indivisible reality.[38] The result is that Tertullian bequeathed to the Western church the terminology for God that is still largely normative for it: God is three persons in one divine substance.

Throughout the third century, emerging trinitarian faith continued to be shaped by necessary orthodox responses to two inadequate understandings of God. One such misguided tendency was to subordinate the Son and the Spirit to the Father, making the Son and the Spirit somehow less fully divine. This heresy is known as *subordinationism.* The other, which we have already encountered in the views of Praxeas and his followers, was the effort to guard the oneness of God by denying the real distinction between each of the three persons. This heresy is known as *modalism.* Modalists believed that Father, Son, and Spirit are only "modes" or aspects of the one divine being. They are ways God's deity is expressed or manifested in God's work in time and

---

[37] Tertullian, *On Modesty*, 21; see A. Roberts and J. Donaldson, eds., *Ante-Nicene Fathers* (Peabody, Mass.: Hendricksen Publishers, 1994), 4:99.

[38] Tertullian, *Against Praxeas*, esp. 2, 9, 11–13, 25; see Roberts and Donaldson, *Ante-Nicene Fathers,* 3:597–627.

creation. But Father, Son, and Spirit do not exist eternally as the threefold divine reality. God only looks or acts like three persons. But this threeness is not finally real. This view was sometimes encouraged by the fact that in both Greek and Latin, the words for *person* (Greek: *prosopon,* Latin: *persona*) often referred to a "face" or even a "mask" used for playing a dramatic role. So these terms could unfortunately obscure the New Testament claims about the authentic, eternal, and intrinsic deity of the Father, Son, and Holy Spirit.)

It took time to recognize the long-term problems to which these views could lead. Even early church thinkers with the most orthodox of motivations were obliged to sort out the negative potential consequences of these ideas gradually, as their effects on the church's faith and confidence came to light in Christian living and worship. If subordinationism were embraced, then the Son and the Spirit would not be fully divine in the same sense as the Father. God's unity would be protected, but at the expense of the New Testament confidence that in the incarnation, suffering, death, and resurrection of Jesus Christ, *it was really God* who had entered the creation and human life physically and tangibly to procure human salvation once and for all. Likewise, the New Testament confidence that in the outpouring of the Holy Spirit, *it is really God* who continues to live in the church and human hearts would be obscured.

On the other hand, if modalism were embraced, the divine unity would be preserved by blurring or dissolving the genuine distinction between God the Father, God the Son, and God the Holy Spirit. In this case, God's oneness would be guarded at the expense of the New Testament confidence that in the incarnation, suffering, death, and resurrection of Jesus Christ, *God had really entered the creation and human life physically and tangibly* to procure human salvation once and for all. Similarly, the New Testament confidence that in the outpouring of the Holy Spirit, *God really continues to live within the church and human hearts* would be diminished.

As these issues were clarified, it became clearer that if *either* subordinationism or modalism were allowed, Christians would have no assurance that in the Father, Son, and Holy Spirit, we genuinely encounter God's very own self. Instead, we would be left with something disappointingly less: divine representatives, or divine manifestations, or divine facades, or even mere ways of thinking about God. By the end of the third century, however, these dangers were still only beginning to be appreciated. Elements of subordinationism and modalism lingered in even the most profound trinitarian reflections of church theologians.

### Jesus Christ: "Of the Same Reality as the Father"

*God from God, Light from Light, true God from true God, begotten, not created, of the same reality as the Father, through him all things were made.*

Nicene Creed, 325

In the early fourth century, a number of these crucial issues came to focus when a popular leader named Arius burst upon the church's awareness in Alexandria in northern Egypt. He made the defiant claim that only the one, eternal, invisible God is without beginning. As a consequence, Arius argued, Jesus Christ, the Son of God, must have been begotten from God as an act of the divine will. The Son had a beginning before which he did not exist. Arius claimed to believe that the Son was "fully God, only-begotten, unchangeable." But at the same time, he insisted that "before he was begotten or created . . . , he did not exist." In contrast to God, who is "without a beginning," the Son did have a beginning.[39]

The internal inconsistencies between Arius's statements about the Son were considerable. How could Christ be "fully God" and also created? If the Son has a beginning and can be called "created," he cannot properly be God in the same sense that Arius's "Unbegotten" is God.

---

[39] Arius, "Letter to Eusebius, Bishop of Nicomedia" (c. 321); see Henry Bettenson, *Documents of the Christian Church,* 2nd ed. (New York: Oxford University Press, 1971), 39.

Though not a particularly clear thinker, Arius was an immensely persuasive popular communicator. There has been much debate about his motives. Some believe he wanted to guard the unity and majesty of God. Others suggest he was trying to make the gospel relevant to everyday life by protecting a particular understanding of human salvation centered in the sense that only Christ as a human being—created like other human beings by an act of the divine will—could fully identify with and thus save humans in our createdness. Whatever the truth is, it is clear that Arius thought of divinity and humanity as fundamentally incompatible, and that this dichotomy controlled what he taught about God and Christ. In the early fourth century, Arianism swept like wildfire throughout the eastern half of the Roman Empire. Arius himself is said to have expressed his key beliefs in popular songs that were picked up by the masses. At the height of the controversy, people are reported to have gone about in the streets of Alexandria shouting "There was when he was not" in Greek,[40] a quote that summarized how Arius's view of Christ differed from the orthodox view.

At just the time that the Arian controversy was at its height, the Roman Empire reversed its stance toward the Christian faith. Under the emperor Constantine, it was formally recognized as an approved religion. This gave the church's theological debates a political dimension, which was eventually crucial in resolving the debate about Arianism. Convinced that religious unity was necessary to achieve the political unity he sought in his realm, Constantine called a universal church council at Nicaea in northwestern Asia Minor in 325 to resolve the conflict. His motives were pragmatic and political, not theological. But under the heavy hand of his imperial leadership, an enduring and broadly embraced statement of trinitarian faith was forged.

Due to its politicized climate, there was great pressure at Nicaea to produce a compromise document. Over the course of the meetings, three distinct groups formed around different posi-

---

[40] Justo González, *A History of Christian Thought,* vol. 1 (Nashville: Abingdon Press, 1987), 265.

tions. A few favored a position similar to that of Arius, who had already been excommunicated, but whose followers continued to multiply. On the other hand, there were many representatives, led by bishop Alexander of Alexandria, who regarded Arianism to be a complete capitulation of Christian faith. In the middle was the majority, which understood what was at stake only partially, and which sought a compromise for pragmatic reasons. The compromise party realized Arius's position was inadequate, and was willing to say that the Son is "of like reality" (Greek: *homoiousion*) with the Father. However, they were sympathetic enough with the problems Arius had raised to be hesitant to say that he was "of the same reality" (Greek: *homoousion*) with the Father. Because the tiny difference between the two Greek words made such an huge difference theologically, the discussion surrounding the Council of Nicaea is sometimes wryly referred to as "the debate over a single *iota*" (the Greek letter transliterated as "i").

Influenced by the prior teachings of Clement of Alexandria and Origen, Alexander and the bishops who supported his position held on the authority of scripture that the Son is eternal, not created but eternally being generated or "begotten" of the Father, and without beginning. He is Son, not by adoption, but by nature. He was not made and has always existed.

After much discussion and controversy—and under the strong urging of Constantine to come to a unified position—this group's theological arguments finally persuaded most of the middle group. The Nicene Creed that was formulated by the council is as follows:

We believe in one God, the Father all-governing,
Creator of all things both visible and invisible.
And in one Lord Jesus Christ, the Son of God,
born of the Father as only-begotten;
that is, from the reality [or "being": *ousia*] of the Father.
God from God, Light from Light, true God from true God;
begotten, not created,
of the same reality [*homoousion*] as the Father;
through him all things were made, both in heaven and on earth.
For us and for our salvation,
he came down and was incarnate, becoming human.

He suffered and the third day he rose, and ascended into heaven.
And he will come to judge both the living, and the dead.
And we believe in the Holy Spirit.
As for those who say:
"There was a time when he was not"
or "before he was begotten, He did not exist,"
or "He was made from nothing,"
or "He, the Son of God, is of another *hypostasis* or reality,"
or that he is a creature, or mutable, or subject to change—
the Catholic and apostolic Church condemns them.[41]

Another influential church leader named Athanasius—a pastor and eventually bishop of Alexandria—had become convinced even before the Council of Nicaea that the entire saving power of the Christian gospel was at stake in Arius's challenge. As a young deacon, he had attended the council with Bishop Alexander, whose position he supported. There he had spoken strongly in favor of the *homoousion* clause that became the focus of the controversy. But the council's statement had not automatically changed public opinion about Arianism or about the relationship of the Son to the Father. In fact, both numerical and political dominance in the empire wavered repeatedly between Arianism and Nicene Christianity throughout the first half of the fourth century.

In this climate of confusion, Athanasius set about to refute and overcome the teaching of Arius. Both were firmly committed to the divine oneness. But Athanasius differed sharply from Arius in his understanding of salvation in Christ. Athanasius was convinced of the devastating impact of our sin on our human capacity to live as God intended and to know the true God. As a result, he was equally certain that only one who was fully and completely God in every way could accomplish our salvation.

On the basis of New Testament teaching and his own extensive pastoral ministry, Athanasius was convinced that human salvation

---

[41] Philip Schaff, ed., *The Creeds of Christendom,* vol. 1 (Grand Rapids: Baker Book House, 1985), 57–58, my translation.

depends completely on the Christian confession that the eternal, immortal Word of God actually assumed human flesh and blood in the incarnation of Jesus Christ. This means that this Word, the Son, must share in the reality of God the Father in such a way that the two are both one and the same God. The Father and the Son are of one identical reality (Greek: *ousia*). The Creator of all must bring the new creation into human existence by embodying that new creation in human flesh. Therefore, the Son could not be created. Instead, the Son is begotten of the Father by an eternal generation that occurs mysteriously by nature and not by will. Athanasius was confident that this was exactly what the New Testament presented as the Christian gospel. It was not merely a theoretical necessity. It was a historical reality. It is God who saves us. Therefore, Christ is and must be "of the same reality" with God.

## The Holy Spirit in the Trinity

*Since [the Spirit] is by nature holy, as the Father is holy by nature, and so is the Son, we do not allow him to be separated and divided from the divine and blessed Trinity.*

Basil of Caesarea[42]

It should not be surprising that in the years following the Council of Nicaea, a parallel controversy developed over the divinity of the Holy Spirit. Various Egyptian church leaders began to sound an ironically familiar theme, now teaching that the Spirit was a creature created from nothing, a ministering spirit similar but superior to angels. Athanasius was still alive, and wrote a series of letters to his friend Serapion, which upheld the Spirit's deity in terms similar to those used against the Arians. The divinity of the Spirit is parallel to the divinity of the Son. Our

---

[42] Basil, Letter 159.2, *Nicene and Post-Nicene Fathers,* ed. P. Schaff and W. Nevin (Peabody, Mass.: Hendricksen, 1994), 8:212.

transformation into the divine image depends on the fully divine, uncreated Spirit's presence and work within created human lives. A Spirit who was a mere creature could certainly not enable human beings to "become participants of the divine nature," as scripture promises (2 Peter 1:4). To the contrary, the Spirit, like the Son, is "of the same reality *(homoousion)* with the Father."[43]

During the same period, a godly bishop from Asia Minor, Basil of Caesarea, did a great deal to make the church more fully aware of the implications of the Spirit's full divinity. Basil argued, "The Lord has delivered to us a necessary and saving dogma: the Holy Spirit is to be ranked with the Father."[44] Basil developed with great insight the characteristic work of the divine Spirit in the church and the believer. But an even greater contribution was to argue for the Spirit's equal place in the Trinity, from the Christian experience of God in baptism and worship, and from the confession of God in the creed.

> We glorify the Holy Spirit together with the Father and the Son, from the conviction that he is not separated from the divine nature; for that which is foreign by nature does not share in the same honors.[45]

Our entire salvation is at stake in the determination to "keep the Spirit undivided from the Father and the Son, preserving, both in the confession of faith and in the doxology, the doctrine taught [at] baptism."[46]

The Nicene Creed of 325 had ended abruptly with the terse phrase, "And we believe in the Holy Spirit." This was no longer all that needed to be said. Efforts to more fully articulate the place of the Spirit in the Trinity, the church, and in the life of believers

---

[43] Athanasius, *Four Letters to Serapion* 1.2, 27; 3.1; see the translation by C. R. B. Shapland, *The Letter of Athanasius Concerning the Holy Spirit* (London: Epworth Press, 1951).

[44] Basil, *On the Holy Spirit* 10 (26); see the translation by D. Anderson (Crestwood, N.Y.: St. Vladimir's Seminary Press, 1980), 46.

[45] Basil, Letter 159, *Nicene and Post-Nicene Fathers,* ed. P. Schaff and W. Nevin (Peabody, Mass.: Hendricksen, 1994), 8:212.

[46] Basil, *On the Holy Spirit* 10 (27); ibid., 47.

were made in various creedal statements from a variety of church worship settings throughout the mid-fourth century. By the Council of Constantinople in 381—upon which Basil's ideas had significant influence—a version of the creed was supported, which was later ratified by the Council of Chalcedon (451) as the "faith of Nicaea." From Chalcedon on, this creed was (somewhat confusingly) called the "Nicene Creed." It has been passed down over the centuries, and is the most widely embraced ecumenical creed and the most authoritative articulation of trinitarian faith ever formulated. It is still confessed in worship at the Eucharist in most historic Christian faith traditions. It echoes many of the crucial ideas found in the Nicene Creed of 325, but contains significant new material, and expresses a number of the earlier Nicene ideas in somewhat different terms. This creed articulates the following more specific statement about the Holy Spirit:

> . . . And in the Holy Spirit, the Lord, the Giver of Life;
> who proceeds from the Father.
> Who with the Father and the Son together is worshiped and glorified.
> Who spoke through the prophets.

3

# Establishment and Clarification

*T*he formal trinitarian statements of the fourth century continue to be crucial in guiding and informing Christian faith right up to the present. They command a broad and historic ecumenical consensus that cannot be claimed by any other trinitarian statements before or since. But these statements did not close discussion on what it means to say that God is triune. Instead, the fresh theological challenges posed by new situations continued to call forth further reflection on trinitarian faith. In the period from the Council of Nicaea in 325 through the Protestant Reformation of the sixteenth century, trinitarian faith was established and clarified as the faith of the New Testament and the Christian church.

### "The Three" as the One God

*No sooner do I conceive of the One than I am illumined by the splendor of the Three; no sooner do I distinguish Them than I am carried back to the One. . . . When I contemplate the Three together, I see but one torch, and cannot divide or measure out the Undivided Light.*
Gregory of Nazianzus, 330–389[1]

In the years following the Council of Nicaea, three distinguished fourth-century Christian bishops assumed a

---

[1] *On Holy Baptism*, Oration 40:41. *Nicene and Post-Nicene Fathers,* ed. P. Schaff and W. Nevin (Peabody, Mass.: Hendricksen, 1994), 7:375.

major role in establishing trinitarian faith. Their most significant writing and teaching took place in the ten years before and the period just after the Council of Constantinople in 381. Together they are known as "the Great Cappadocians," after Cappadocia, the region of Asia Minor (modern Turkey) in which they conducted their pastoral ministries. The first of these to influence trinitarian thought was Basil of Caesarea, whose early contribution toward recognition of the full deity of the Holy Spirit we have already noted at the end of chapter 2. The other two were Gregory of Nyssa, Basil's brother, and Gregory of Nazianzus, their friend. After Basil's death in 379, Gregory of Nazianzus and Gregory of Nyssa continued to reinforce the importance of affirming the full deity of the Spirit, freely stating that the Spirit is God and is "of the same reality" as the Father. Their influence at the 381 Council of Constantinople was crucial to its final result.

After the Council of Nicaea in 325, a pressing need to agree upon a single term for the divine unity and another, distinct term for the Three had emerged. The Cappadocians' starting point was the New Testament confidence that Father, Son, and Holy Spirit were each divine in some mysterious way that did not contradict God's oneness. The question that consumed their attention was: If the Father, Son, and Holy Spirit are a single divine reality, how do we refer to their genuine distinctness, and how do we refer to their unity? What term can we use for the threeness, that does not compromise the divine oneness? The challenge was to choose the most suitable available terms from the Greek language and then carefully redefine them for this specialized need, so that the many potential misunderstandings surrounding belief in God's triunity were avoided.

In response to these questions, the Cappadocians enabled the church to agree on the Greek term *hypostasis* for each of the Three: Father, Son, and Holy Spirit. This was a major step, since especially in the eastern part of the empire, there had previously been significant overlap of meaning between the word *hypostasis* and the term agreed upon for referring to the one divine reality: *ousia*.

To the Cappadocians, each *hypostasis*—Father, Son, and Holy Spirit—is fully divine. Each *hypostasis* is also genuinely distinct from the other two, although in no way separate or divided from them. The divine reality or *ousia* is not divided into parts in the three *hypostaseis,* nor is it a "fourth" reality. It does not exist apart from the three divine *hypostaseis*: Father, Son, and Spirit. God is wholly present in each of the Three. In this way, the normative terminology was established for the Greek-speaking eastern half of the Roman Empire that had been defined for the Latin West by Tertullian almost two centuries before. Three divine *hypostaseis* mutually sharing in a single *ousia.*

A year after the Council of Constantinople, a new synod meeting there in 382 formalized this language in the following, fuller trinitarian statement:

> This is the faith which ought to be sufficient for you,
> for us, and for all who do not deny the word of the true faith;
> for it is the ancient faith,
> it is the faith of our baptism;
> it is the faith that teaches us
> to believe in the name of the Father, of the Son, and of the
>     Holy Spirit.
> According to this faith there is one Godhead, power, and sub-
>     stance *(ousia)*
> of the Father and of the Son and of the Holy Spirit;
> equal in honor, majesty, and eternal sovereignty
> in three most perfect subsistences *(hypostaseis);*
> that is, three perfect persons.[2]

As the translation above indicates, the Greek word *ousia* is often translated in English by the word *substance,* from the Latin *substantia* (other English translations include "essence" or "being"). The Greek word *hypostasis* is often translated with the English word *subsistence* (or, drawing on the Latin terminology, "person"). This terminology attempts to clarify the fact that the Three are neither merely individual or sequential manifestations

---

[2] *Nicene and Post-Nicene Fathers,* ed. P. Schaff and W. Nevin (Peabody, Mass.: Hendricksen, 1994), 14:189; cf. Theodoret, *The Ecclesiastical History,* ibid., 3:138; translation with my emendations from the Greek.

of God in time (this would be modalism), nor discrete species of a broader category with the generic name "God" (this would suggest three Gods). Instead, because we know from the biblical narrative that God the Father has entered human existence in the Son, and that God lives in human community and human lives as Holy Spirit, we can say that Father, Son, and Holy Spirit are the three distinct but inseparable ways in which the one God, identical in the three persons, exists as God.

Once suitable terminology for "the Three" in relationship to "the One" had been established, the question of how the Three are distinct from each other had to be addressed. The Cappadocians, and particularly Gregory of Nazianzus, clarified an idea that had already been suggested by others. The three *hypostaseis*, he suggested, are distinguished from one another by their unique relationships of origin with each other. The terminology the Cappadocians adopted was drawn largely from the Gospel of John, and reflects the intuitive implications of the Father-Son relationship that is prominent in the New Testament. In response to Arianism, the creeds had already emphasized that the Father alone is "unbegotten" or "ungenerated." The Son, then, is distinguished from the Father in that he is "only begotten" or "uniquely generated" from the Father (John 1:18, 3:16; Col. 1:15; cf. Ps. 2:7; Heb. 1:5). Emphasizing this idea of divine begetting—a term associated with the male role in the reproductive process—helped to clarify the fact that the Son was uncreated and was of the same reality or substance as the Father.[3] However, this divine begetting had to be distinguished from the ideas of Arius, so it was carefully emphasized that the Son was "*eternally* begotten" from the Father, rather than having been begotten at some point in time. This avoided the implication that the Son had a beginning. In

---

[3] In Christian tradition, "Fatherhood" in the Trinitarian sense does not entail any assumption of male gender or male sexuality in God. This awareness received remarkable expression in the statement of the Council of Toledo in 675: "It must be held that the Son was created, neither out of nothingness nor yet out of any substance, but that he was begotten or born out of the Father's womb (*de utero Patris*), that is, out of his very essence." Cited in J. Moltmann, *The Trinity and the Kingdom* (San Francisco: Harper & Row, 1981), 165.

turn, the Spirit eternally "proceeds" from the Father (John 15:26) in such a way that the Spirit has no beginning either. Gregory of Nyssa put it more simply, but less precisely, with these words:

> [T]he persons of the Godhead are not divided from each other in time, place, will, occupation, activity or any qualifications of the sort, the distinguishing marks observed in human beings. The only distinction here is that the Father is father, not son: the Son is son, not father; similarly, the Holy Spirit is neither father nor son.[4]

The Cappadocians also devoted much thought to the question of how the three *hypostaseis* are one God. In their efforts to conceptualize and explain the profound mystery of Trinitarian unity, they proposed a number of analogies. Gregory of Nyssa suggested a torch lighting another torch, which in turn gives its light to a third torch. Sometimes they spoke of three individual human beings who are united in one common nature. Gregory of Nazianzus, however, saw the need to contrast the merely conceptual and generic unity that exists between three people (because they share a common class as "humanity") with the real or substantial unity that characterizes the Trinity. He speaks in paradox: the Godhead exists "undivided . . . in divided *hypostaseis*." "To us there is One God, for the Godhead is One, and all that proceeds from him is referred to One, though we believe in three *hypostaseis*." Searching for an illustration, he suggests "one mingling of Light, as it were of three suns joined to each other."[5]

Sometimes the Cappadocians appealed to what they called "the Monarchy" of the Father as the basis of the unity of the Trinity. This idea builds on the original one of the Nicene Council of 325 that the Father generates the Son and Spirit from the Father's

---

[4] Gregory of Nyssa, *On Common Notions; Against the Greeks*; cited in Henry Bettenson, *Later Christian Fathers* (London: Oxford University Press, 1974), 158.

[5] Gregory of Nazianzus, *Oration* 34:14; the English translation is from *Nicene and Post-Nicene Fathers,* ed. P. Schaff and W. Nevin (Peabody, Mass.: Hendricksen, 1994), 7:322.

own being.[6] Another approach, stated most sharply by Gregory of Nyssa, was to find the divine oneness of the Father, Son, and Holy Spirit in the inseparability of the divine activity in the world: "We are not told that the Father does anything by himself in which the Son does not cooperate; or that the Son has any isolated activity, apart from the Holy Spirit." "Every [divine] activity originates from the Father, proceeds through the Son, and is brought to fulfillment in the Holy Spirit."[7]

But the Cappadocians' most interesting and enduring contribution to understanding the divine unity was their tendency to think of the Father, Son, and Holy Spirit as *being in* each other, and *dwelling in* each other. This thought was suggested by various texts in the Gospel of John.[8] The Cappadocians emphasized that each of the Three exists in each of the others mutually. Because of the one *ousia,* in each *hypostasis* the other two are completely and wholly present. Other Christian theologians such as Hilary of Poiters (315–367) and Cyril of Alexandria (d. 444) further explored and expressed this important understanding of divine oneness. Later, John of Damascus (675–749) classically stated it, saying that the *hypostaseis* "have their being in one another," yet "without any coalescence or commingling."[9] As the idea developed, it included the sense that each *hypostasis* is contained in the others. Each permeates the others. Each inhabits the others. They are coterminous and coextensive. Eventually, this subtle explanation of the divine oneness came to be called *perichoresis* or *coinherence.* It was a very important step forward in more deeply articulating how the Father, Son, and Holy Spirit together are one God. This idea of *perichoresis* has had enduring appeal throughout the church's history, especially in the Eastern churches. Today, many contemporary Western theologians are

---

[6] Gregory of Nazianzus, *Oration* 50:41 (*On Holy Baptism*); see *Nicene and Post-Nicene Fathers,* ed. P. Schaff and W. Nevin (Peabody, Mass.: Hendricksen, 1994), 7:375.

[7] Gregory of Nyssa, *That There Are Not Three Gods,* quoted in Bettenson, *Later Christian Fathers,* 153.

[8] John 14:10–11, 20; 15:15; 17:10–11, 21–23.

[9] John of Damascus, *On the Orthodox Faith,* 1.8; trans. F. C. Chase (Washington, D.C.: Catholic University of America Press, 1958).

gaining important trinitarian insights from this approach also, as we will see in the next chapter.

Although they believed it was crucial to continue to seek to articulate the trinitarian mystery as clearly as possible, the Cappadocians shared a mutual recognition that human language is ultimately inadequate to fully comprehend divine reality. We can never "wrap our minds around" God. As Gregory of Nyssa expressed it:

> Following the instructions of Holy Scripture, we have been taught that [the nature of God] is beyond human names or human speech. We say that all references to divinity, whether derived from purely human resources or transmitted to us in the scriptures, expresses what we may understand of the divine nature, but does not contain the essence itself.[10]

Trinitarian faith in the Eastern Orthodox tradition has continued to develop along the basic lines of thought originally suggested by the Cappadocians, including a humble awareness of the limitations of human language in speaking of divine realities.

## One God in Three Persons

*We shall endeavor to give an explanation [of the fact] that the Trinity is the one, only, and true God, and that one rightly says, believes, and understands that the Father, the Son, and the Holy Spirit are of one and the same substance or essence.*

Augustine, c. 416[11]

In the Latin-speaking West, appreciation of the significance of the Cappadocian insights had been delayed by differences in lan-

---

[10] Gregory of Nyssa, *That There Are Not Three Gods*; cf. the English translation in *Nicene and Post-Nicene Fathers,* ed. P. Schaff and W. Nevin (Peabody, Mass.: Hendricksen 1994), 5:332.

[11] *The Trinity*, trans. Stephen McKenna (Washington, D.C.: Catholic University of America Press, 1963), 7.

guage and thought, as well as by distance. Hilary, writing about 360, was a significant influence in bringing ideas and terminology developed in the Eastern discussions into the stream of Latin theological awareness. But it was Augustine, bishop of Hippo in North Africa, who gave Western trinitarian faith its fullest and most definitive expression in the early fifth century.

If the Cappadocians were concerned to explain how the Father, Son, and Holy Spirit of the New Testament could be one God, Augustine approached the trinitarian challenge from the opposite direction. As he considered the Trinity, he began with the basic assumption of God's oneness. Before becoming a Christian, Augustine had believed the Manichaean idea of two equal divine forces, one good and the other evil. It was his conversion to the conviction that all existence stands under the ultimate sovereignty and goodness of one unique and all-powerful God that had enabled him to embrace Christianity. How could this one God exist in three distinct Persons?

Augustine's challenge was complicated by the fact that the Latin terms which Tertullian's usage had standardized in the West (one substance [*substantia*] in three persons [*personae*]) did not correspond precisely with the normal translations of the now definitive Greek terms (three *hypostaseis* in one *ousia*). In fact, the Greek term *hypostasis* was usually rendered in Latin with *substantia*. It would not be until 451 at the Council of Chalcedon that the church would officially declare *hypostasis* and *persona* to be equivalent.

Augustine had a profound awareness of the linguistic difficulties. But he believed the best available terminology must be used "in order that we not remain silent." With deep sensitivity to the limitations of human words and concepts, he nevertheless concluded that the unity of the Trinity consists in the identical divine essence shared by each person (he preferred the term "essence" to "substance" because of the difficulty in translating the latter). It is not that one substance unfolds or takes expression in three forms. "There is nothing else of this divine essence beside the Trinity."[12] The three persons are not *from* the same essence. They

12 Augustine, *Trinity*, 238.

*are* that same essence without remainder. At the same time, each of the divine persons is fully and intrinsically God. No divine person receives deity from another divine person; instead, each of the divine Persons is completely equal: "Each person of the Trinity is God, and all together are One God. Each is the full essence, and all together are one essence."[13] "In God to be is not one thing, and to be a person another thing, but it is wholly and entirely one and the same."[14]

According to Augustine, when scripture says "God" without specifying a particular divine person, the whole Trinity is meant. "What is said about each one in the Trinity is likewise said about all of them, on account of the inseparable activity of the one and the same substance."[15] Everything the triune God does with respect to the creation and human beings is the united work of the whole Trinity, accomplished by means of a single divine will and activity.

Augustine did not reject the Cappadocian tendency to express the distinction of the persons in terms of relations of origin: generation in the case of the Son, procession in the case of the Spirit. But in his efforts to avoid any kind of subordinationism, he moved into new territory. He was more inclined to think of the distinction of the persons in terms of the present relationships between them. Both God's identity and God's work are indivisibly one, not triple. So the distinction between the divine persons can in no way be based on differing roles or functions reflected in their work in the world. The persons can only be distinguished from each other relationally (the Father in relationship to the Son, the Son in relationship to the Father, the Spirit in relationship to the Father and the Son). God is one according to essence; three according to relation.

This approach to the distinction of persons works well in the case of the Father and the Son. It is not hard to see that the Father

---

[13] Augustine, *On Christian Doctrine,* 1:5; cf. the English translation by D. W. Robertson, Jr. (Indianapolis: Bobbs-Merrill Co. Inc., 1958), 10. I have made my own emendations with reference to the Latin.
[14] Augustine, *Trinity,* 235–36.
[15] Ibid., 37.

might be relationally distinguished from the other two persons by virtue of being the Father of the Son. Neither is it difficult to recognize that the Son might be relationally distinguished from the other two persons by virtue of being the Son of the Father. For Augustine, it was precisely this relationship that accounts for the distinction of these two persons. The Father is not the Son, and the Son is not the Father.

But this logic is not as clear in the case of the Holy Spirit, who does not have an intuitively obvious relationship to either the Father or Son that can be derived from the term "Holy Spirit" itself. So Augustine developed a suggestion from his predecessor Marius Victorinus, and filled it out with his own characteristic emphasis on love. The Father is the One who loves (the Son). The Son is the Beloved, the One who is loved (by the Father). The Spirit is the bond of love between them. Augustine can also speak of the mutual love of the Father and the Son, and of the Spirit as the Gift of love that comes from and is given to each by the other. In this formulation, the Spirit constitutes the divine unity as the communion of the Father and Son. Furthermore, the Spirit's distinction from the Father and the Son is precisely as the love that issues from both the Father and the Son. This latter train of thought leads to the idea of the *double procession* of the Holy Spirit from both the Father and the Son. This idea later created great tension between the Eastern and Western traditions of Christianity and eventually contributed to their separation, as we will see.

Like the Cappadocians, with whose work he was only indirectly familiar through Hilary, Augustine invested a great deal of effort in developing analogies for the Trinity. But instead of choosing analogies that made use of three entities and sought to cast light on their oneness, Augustine favored analogies that distinguish three facets of a single reality, analogies that could thus illustrate how the one God could subsist in three persons. Based on the assumption that each human being is created in and reflects the image of the triune God as an individual, he reasoned that the human individual is the best source of trinitarian analogies. Consequently, most of the analogies he developed most seriously reflect inner (or "psychological") aspects within a single human being. This choice had enormous influence on the later history of Western trinitarian faith, and the Western view of God. He considered many analogies like this: being, knowing, and willing; the mind, its self-knowledge, and its self-love; memory, understanding, and will; and the mind remembering, understanding, and loving God. Augustine's influence on the shape of trinitarian faith was so immense that until recent times, all Western trinitarian discussion has been obliged to take its bearings from him. In the centuries just after he wrote, others tried to sharpen his reflection on the precise meaning of the term *person* with reference to God. Boethius (c. 480–c. 524) was greatly influenced by Aristotle's philosophy. In discussing the Trinity, he defined *person* as "an individual substance of a rational nature." This definition became immensely influential throughout the Middle Ages. But as the philosophical meanings of these ideas changed over time, it tended to complicate rather than clarify the articulation and understanding of trinitarian faith. On the one hand, it could be misunderstood as if the persons of the Trinity are simply individual instances of a common class. On the other hand, it could obscure the established terminology, since in Boethius's definition the idea of "substance" is associated individually with each of the Three, whereas both the Cappadocians and Augustine had been careful to reserve this idea to express God's uniqueness and unity.

### Eastern and Western Trinitarian Trajectories

*. . . And in the Holy Spirit . . . who proceeds from the Father.*
The original and Eastern version of the Nicene Creed, 381

*. . . And in the Holy Spirit . . . who proceeds from the Father and from the Son.*
The Western version of the Nicene Creed, c. 800

Enduring tensions eventually developed between the Cappadocian approach, which was most influential in the Greek-speaking Eastern church, and the Augustinian approach, which was most influential in the Latin-speaking Western church. The Eastern approach tended to begin with the New Testament assertion that Father, Son, and Spirit were each divine, and to concentrate on understanding and explaining how these three could be one. If pursued in an unbalanced way, the danger of this approach was the impression of three Gods, or the subordination of the Son and Spirit to the Father who was viewed as their "cause." On the other hand, the Western approach tended to assume and emphasize the divine oneness, working to understand and explain how the one God could exist in three persons. In its concern to guard the divine unity, this approach raised the danger of dissolving the genuine distinctions between the Three, as had occurred in earlier modalism. The new religion of Islam was rising rapidly. It centered in the uncompromising assertion of the divine oneness, explicitly repudiating the Trinity as the worship of three Gods. Awareness of these criticisms increased the inclination of Western Christians to emphasize God's oneness and to be cautious about emphasizing genuine distinctions between the Three. In later Western Christian thought, these concerns were reflected in a strong emphasis on monotheism (stress on the importance of God's oneness and eventually also on God's "transcendence": God's unknowability and utter unlikeness to the created world). These emphases greatly affected Western Christian conceptions of God and Christian worship and devotion, as we will see.

This difference is illustrated in the very different depictions of the Trinity that developed in religious art in the East and West. In the East, religious icons, or images, were cherished as aids to Christian worship and devotion. They were believed to help the worshiper focus adoration on the divine reality reflected in and through the image. In Eastern art, the Trinity was characteristically depicted as three individuals (traditionally associated with the three "guests" who visited Abraham and Sarah in Genesis 18), seated around a table, which evoked the Christian sacrament of Communion or Eucharist. This image suggested the Eastern idea that the divine unity consists in the intimate communion and fellowship of the Three. The Greek word for this communion was *koinonia*, a rich term that suggested mutual participation in and sharing of divine life, love, and goodness. As this visual image informed Eastern worship and devotion over the centuries, it contributed immeasurably to the emphasis on *perichoresis*, or mutual interaction and intimate sharing and self-giving, as the way the three persons together are one God. Eventually, it led to a willingness in Eastern trinitarian faith to connect the idea of *hypostasis* with the modern idea of a "person" as a distinct personality, living in intimate intercommunion with the other two divine "persons."[16] This, of course, was a very different understanding of "person" than the original Latin and Greek sense of "appearance" or "visage" or even "mask," a definition that had originally emphasized the divine oneness.

Western liturgical art was originally more hesitant to depict the Trinity. This hesitation arose from the Old Testament concern that visual images of the invisible God tempt the worshiper to idolatry. However, a number of Western artistic depictions of the Trinity survive. These follow Augustine's analogies in depicting distinct aspects of a single human being. This, in turn, encouraged addressing worship and prayer to the One God, without specific mention of the three divine persons. In the West, if the modern idea of personality were to be applied to God at all, it would normally be to the one divine reality. Prayer or direct devotion addressed toward just one of the three persons individually has sometimes even been discouraged, in spite of the human Jesus' own example, and against abundant additional New Testament examples of such prayer and devotion.

A second issue, which ultimately encouraged a divisive disagreement between the Eastern and Western branches of the church, was the question of the procession of the Holy Spirit. Did the Holy Spirit proceed from the Father and the Son together as one principle, as Augustine had taught, and as Western Christians gradually came to believe? Or did the Holy Spirit proceed from

---

[16] See Vladimir Lossky, *The Mystical Theology of the Eastern Church* (London: James Clarke & Co., 1957), 53.

the Father alone, *through* the Son, as Eastern Christians continued to teach and believe?

This issue took center stage in the period from the ninth through the eleventh centuries, for two reasons. First, as the bishop of Rome made stronger and stronger claims to be the one head of the whole church, the Western church asserted its position by adding the phrase "and from the Son" to the version of the Nicene Creed that it used as the official standard of belief for the whole church. The resulting statement about the Holy Spirit was as follows:

> We believe in the Holy Spirit, the Lord, the Giver of Life, who proceeds from the Father *and from the Son*; who with the Father and the Son together is worshiped and glorified.

The phrase "and from the Son" (in Latin this phrase was expressed in the single word *filioque)* had not been present in the original creed of 381 that was agreed upon at Constantinople and approved in 451 at Chalcedon as the official profession of faith of the catholic church.

In addition to the political resentment this unilateral move created in the East, theological concerns were also raised by the influential theologian Photius (c. 810–897). Photius defended the Cappadocian teaching of the "Monarchy" of the Father, the view that the Father was sole cause of the Son and the Spirit. His writings strongly emphasized that just as the Son is begotten of the Father alone, the Spirit proceeds from the Father alone. The Spirit proceeds *through* the Son, but not *from* the Son.

In response to these political and theological concerns, the Eastern churches refused to incorporate the Roman revision into the Greek version of the creed that summarized their faith. The West insisted that they do so, claiming the universal authority of the pope over the faith of the whole church. Provoked by this and other differences, the Western and Eastern branches split into separate Roman Catholic and Eastern Orthodox Churches in 1054, mutually excommunicating each other. Again, the significance of trinitarian language had been illustrated by the power of a single word to lead to an immense and longstanding disagreement within the Christian church.

## Reason and Faith in Trinitarian Reflection

*[W]hen we would show forth the truth of the blessed Trinity . . . we start with acceptance, and then afterwards may give recommending reasons, without presuming that they sufficiently demonstrate the mystery.*
Thomas Aquinas, 1225–1274[17]

In the high medieval culture of Western Europe, trinitarian faith was explored in profound new depths. In some cases, this revived emphasis on the Trinity reflected optimism about the God-given power of reverent human reason to probe divine realities. But it could also be a way of expressing faithful reverence and devotion for the revealed mystery of God.

The first important medieval approach to trinitarian faith we will consider was that of Peter Lombard (c. 1100–1160). Lombard's summary of Christian doctrine, the *Books of the Sentences*, became a standard Roman Catholic theological textbook for five centuries. He valued tradition and orthodoxy more than theological creativity or logical consistency. Writing before the high medieval theologies of the thirteenth century, Lombard reflected a trinitarian understanding of God in intentional continuity with the early church. To talk about God at all was to talk about God as Father, Son, and Holy Spirit. In contrast with Eastern thinkers, he showed a special concern to avoid the implication that either the divine essence or the person of the Father generated the essence of the Son and the Spirit. Instead, he emphasized the self-existence of the divine essence in each of the divine persons. Generation and procession applied only to the divine persons as persons: the Father generating the person of the Son, and the Father and the Son together generating the person of the Holy Spirit.

---

[17] *Summa Theologica* 1a.32.1, ad 2, quoted from *Theological Texts* (Durham: Labyrinth, 1982), 43.

Richard of St. Victor (d. 1173), a monk whose ideas developed in a monastery renowned for its traditions of theological reflection, began a trinitarian trajectory that was eventually expanded in the systematic development of Bonaventure. To Richard, the Trinity was "the supreme article of our faith."[18] Clarifying Boethius's now classic definition, he spoke of a divine person as "an incommunicable existence of the divine nature." In the effort to prove the existence of a second and a third person in God, Richard developed a fresh understanding of the Trinity as a community of love, drawing on the biblical statement in John's letters that "God is love." To be self-giving love, a divine person must have another, equally divine person with which to share that love. Then rather than being exclusive, this self-giving love will produce another with whom that love continues to be shared: "The affection of the two flows together in the kindling of a third love."[19] Thus, for Richard, the persons exist and are who they are by virtue of their loving communion with one another. This approach had roots in both the Eastern idea of *perichoresis* and in Augustine. But Richard's discussion combined the two approaches in a way that helped to clarify that by their very nature, all three persons exist in and for one another, as a divine community of mutual, self-giving love.

Bonaventure (1217–1274), a Franciscan monk and one of the most profound and visionary systematic thinkers of the Middle Ages, expanded upon this attempt to logically demonstrate the relational necessity for God's triunity. As the highest Good, it is God's nature to share or "diffuse" the divine goodness. The first person of the Trinity does this by way of generation and spiration (breathing forth), producing a beloved (the Son) and a cobeloved (the Spirit).[20] Bonaventure went on to explain all reality and all human progress toward God's presence in expansively trinitarian

[18] See Jaroslav Pelikan, *A History of the Development of Doctrine,* vol. 3 (Chicago: University of Chicago Press, 1978), 279.

[19] E. J. Fortman, *The Triune God* (Grand Rapids: Baker Book House, 1972), 191–94.

[20] Bonaventure, *The Soul's Journey into God,* trans. I. Brady (New York: Paulist Press, 1978), 102ff.

terms. There is a basic trinitarian structure to all created existence (for which he finds evidence in threefold patterns in nature, human personality, the church, society, etc.) that mirrors God's own triunity. These created evidences point to the divine, uncreated Trinity.

Another crucial trajectory of medieval trinitarian reflection extends from Augustine through the Italian Thomas Aquinas (1225–1274), whose logically comprehensive and compelling theological perspective was so influential that it continued to provide the definitive basis for Roman Catholic theology through the middle of the twentieth century. Thomas believed that the existence of the one God could be rationally, or philosophically demonstrated. However, God's triunity could be known only by faith, on the basis of divine revelation in scripture. This led him to separate his discussion of God's existence and attributes from his discussion of God's triunity, giving logical priority to the former. The consequences of this structural choice for later Western belief in God were immense. Thomas affirmed Augustine's teaching that every unspecified mention of "God" in scripture referred to the whole Trinity. But in his theological legacy, the Trinity often became secondary in talk about God. Later theologians and philosophers commonly spoke of God and God's attributes before and without reference to the Trinity. The resulting patterns of worship and devotion reflected a more and more general, abstract understanding of "God," conceived without specific or tangible reference to the New Testament revelation of Father, Son, and Spirit in the gospel story.

Thomas influenced Western trinitarian thought in other significant ways. He gave careful attention to the distinction of the persons. In his commitment to the divine oneness, he extended the ideas of Augustine and Anselm of Canterbury (1033–1109), arguing that the distinction between the persons lies solely and completely in the opposition of relations between them. Thomas could even say, "*Persona est relatio*" (the person is the relation).[21] In order for God's threeness to be properly acknowledged, he was

[21] *Summa Theologica* 1a, 29, a.4.

careful to specify that these must be *real*—not just logical—relations. This idea contrasted significantly with developing Eastern Orthodox perspectives, in which their opposing relationships characterized (rather than being identified with) the divine *hypostaseis.*[22] Whereas earlier (and especially Eastern) thinkers had been content to leave the precise difference between generation and procession in the realm of mystery, Thomas sought to specify it. The Son's generation is a going forth of the divine intellect resulting in One like in nature, whereas the Spirit's procession is a going forth of the divine will, resulting in Love.

Another significant idea to which Thomas gave extended and original attention was that of the divine "missions." This term allowed a distinction to be made between the processions that take place eternally within God's own self, and the sending forth of the Son and the Spirit into the created world in time for human salvation. The missions are motivated by divine grace, and involve a new way of existing within creation and time in order to save human beings and set us apart to enjoy God's own self. Properly speaking, the Father does not have a mission. But the Father does lovingly give self in the missions of the Son and the Spirit, to be freely enjoyed by the creature. The Son's mission is to incarnate the divine being visibly in the world, taking on our human nature for our salvation. The Spirit's mission is to actualize God's love of the creature in particular creatures and signs in the world, imparting God's goodness.[23]

## Divine Motherhood in the Trinity

*God rejoices that he is our Father, and God rejoices that he is our Mother.*

Julian of Norwich, c. 1375

Discussion of the Trinity in the schools of the late medieval period focused on increasingly precise refinement of conceptual

---

[22] Lossky, *The Mystical Theology of the Eastern Church,* 57.
[23] *Summa Theologica* 1a, 43.

distinctions for the purpose of logical clarification. In this same period, a humble English nun with considerable skills in Latin and rhetoric articulated a distinctive understanding of God that harkened back to Old Testament images of God as divine Mother. Julian of Norwich (1342–1423) showed less concern for rigorous theological formulation than for expressing her own mystical experience of a God in intimate relationship with human beings. She did this with a richly feminine and maternal imagery that was not intended to substitute for—but rather to supplement and stretch—traditional trinitarian ideas of God as Father, Son, and Holy Spirit in relationship to Christian believers. Julian associates not the first, but the second person of the Trinity—the divine Word or wisdom—with divine motherhood:

"The high might of the Trinity is our Father, and the deep wisdom of the Trinity is our Mother, and the great love of the Trinity is our Lord."

"In our making, God almighty is our loving Father, and God all wisdom is our loving Mother, with the love and the goodness of the Holy Spirit, which is all one God, one Lord."

"Thus in our Father, God almighty, we have our being, and in our Mother of mercy we have our reforming and our restoring, in whom our parts were united and all made perfect man, and through the rewards and the gifts of grace of the Holy Spirit we are fulfilled."

"Our Father wills, our Mother works, our good Lord the Holy Spirit confirms."[24]

Julian's unique articulation of trinitarian faith reflects her personal perception of God's maternal and feminine care. She remains committed to the traditional naming of the first person of the Trinity as "Father." Her willingness to associate the second person—who became incarnate in the historical male, Jesus the

---

[24] Julian of Norwich, *Showings* (New York: Paulist Press, 1978), cited in *Readings in Christian Thought*, 2d ed., ed. Hugh Kerr (Nashville: Abingdon Press, 1990), 127–29.

Messiah—with divine motherhood is startling. It reflects both Old Testament imagery that depicts God's maternal dealings with human beings in the story of salvation, and New Testament association of the divine Word with divine wisdom, for which the Old Testament had often employed feminine imagery. It provides a fascinating reminder that created categories of gender cannot be simplistically applied either to the triune God's work in the world, or to the internal divine relationships. It also raises a provocative challenge to those who have argued—both then and now—that because God assumed human form in the man Jesus Christ, male gender more closely approximates the divine reality than female gender.

### The Trinitarian Persons as the Focus of Christian Faith

*[We are] baptized into the name of the one God who has shown himself with complete clarity in the Father, the Son, and the Spirit. Hence it is quite clear that in God's essence reside three persons in whom one God is known.*

John Calvin, 1559[25]

The Protestant Reformation of the sixteenth century reflected a renewed focus on God's gracious salvation of human beings by the Holy Spirit, accomplished in the coming of Jesus Christ. The reformers rigorously reevaluated what they perceived as a medieval approach to God bound by deductive and abstract philosophical logic. In their view, this approach tended to make human salvation and relationship with God seem remote and inaccessible to ordinary human beings. In this reevaluation, they returned to scripture—as interpreted in the writings of the orthodox early church theologians—as their primary authority for trinitarian teaching.

Martin Luther (1483–1546) was particularly concerned to emphasize that human attempts to approach or discover God through

[25] *Institutes of the Christian Religion*, ed. J. T. McNeill (Philadelphia: Westminster Press, 1960) 1.13.16.

intellectual reflection or moral accomplishment were futile. Human beings—all of whom participate by nature and their own sin in the original fall from God's immediate favor and presence depicted in the biblical story of Adam and Eve—cannot know God except as God has chosen to reveal God's own self in Jesus Christ:

> Whoever wishes to be saved should leave the majestic God alone—for he and the human creature are enemies. Rather grasp that God whom David (Psalm 51) also grasps. He is the God who is clothed in his promises—God as he is present in Christ. . . . This is the God you need.[26]

In trinitarian terms, their biblical sense of the contrast between the majesty and holiness of God and the depths of human sin encouraged the reformers to focus away from efforts to know or describe God's essence. Rather, their emphasis was on the three divine persons in their gracious, indivisible divine work within creation for the sake of human wholeness and restoration to communion with God.[27]

The second-generation reformer John Calvin (1509–1564) drew together Reformation teaching in his *Institutes of the Christian Religion*.[28] He emphasized that if we conceptualize or worship God as anything beside or less than the Trinity revealed in the New Testament, we commit idolatry. Thus—returning to the approach of Lombard—he did not start with an abstract idea of God and then add on discussion of the Trinity later. Instead, he treated God as thoroughly and completely trinitarian from the beginning. To Calvin, we have no standpoint from which to talk about God at all except as the Father, Son, and Holy Spirit made known in the New Testament. He emphasized the trinitarian per-

---

[26] Cited in Paul Althaus, *The Theology of Martin Luther*, trans. R. Schultz (Philadelphia: Fortress Press, 1966), 20.

[27] For this emphasis and that of the following paragraphs, see Philip W. Butin, *Revelation, Redemption, and Response: Calvin's Trinitarian Understanding of the Divine–Human Relationship* (New York: Oxford University Press, 1995), esp. 26–94; and Gerald Bray, *The Doctrine of God* (Downers Grove, Ill.: InterVarsity Press, 1993), 197–212.

[28] See especially 1.13.

sons' mutual accomplishment of God's saving work in the world, stressing their complete equality. He avoided, as had Lombard, the early idea that the divinity of the Son and the Spirit might derive from that of the Father. The persons are fully divine, each in their own right. The inseparable unity of the persons as the one, identical divine reality is evident from their mutual cooperation and interaction in every divine work in the world. Calvin's relational understanding of the unity of the persons often reflected the Cappadocian idea of *perichoresis*. But his use of this idea was less focused on God's inner life than on God's united trinitarian activity in creating, redeeming, and restoring the world according to the divine purpose.

Calvin devoted particular attention to God's gracious, saving relationship with human beings. God the Father makes the divine nature known to us in Jesus Christ by the Holy Spirit. In this gracious *revelation* of God the Father, the Trinity is the basis of our relationship with God. We are put back in right relationship with the Father through what the divine Son Jesus Christ—the one uniquely anointed with the Holy Spirit—has accomplished for us. In Christ, God assumed human flesh, died on the cross as the sacrifice for our sins, was raised from the dead, and went before us into the Father's immediate presence. In this gracious *redemption* extended in the Son, the Trinity is the pattern of our relationship with God. And God the Father restores the divine image in us as the Spirit unites us to Christ through faith, so that we can freely and authentically say "yes" to God and live in harmony with God's created purpose for us. In enabling genuinely human *response* to God by the Holy Spirit, the Trinity is the dynamic of our relationship with God.

# 4

# Challenge and Recovery

*I*n the period following the Protestant Reformation in Europe, what is now known as the Modern period of Western history came into its own. It was a time of Roman Catholic resurgence, religious wars and persecution, and detailed theological elaboration and defense of Protestant beliefs. In reaction to these developments, the idea of religious tolerance gained influence in European thought. Many turned away from explicit concern about the Trinity, which had been the source of theological disputes in the Reformation that had sometimes led to the persecution and even execution of those who departed from orthodoxy. Gradually, philosophers questioned the reigning assumption of God's centrality. Eventually, this raised new criticisms and posed new challenges for trinitarian faith.

## Doctrinal Refinement and Religious Affections

*[In the new creation] there will be a deep, an intimate, an uninterrupted union with God; a constant communion with the Father and his Son Jesus Christ, through the Spirit; a continual enjoyment of the Three-One God, and of all creatures in him.*

John Wesley, 1785[1]

---

[1] Sermon 64, "The New Creation," in *The Works of John Wesley*, vol. 2, ed. A. Outler (Nashville: Abingdon Press, 1985), 510.

In the seventeenth and early eighteenth centuries, both Protestant and Roman Catholic theological writing about God often returned to the more abstract tone that had characterized the rigorously logical scholastic method of the high and late Middle Ages. In theological circles, it was a period of self-conscious orthodoxy, where the emphasis fell on precise statement of doctrine. In pursuing these concerns, the New Testament focus on the intimate, loving relationship of the Father and the Son, the life-giving and transforming power of the Spirit, and the active work of Father, Son, and Spirit to restore human beings to relationship with God was easily overlooked. As a result, everyday Christians often had limited awareness of the crucial role of the Trinity in Christian faith, worship, and practice.

In England, however, the traditions of Puritanism focused on the transforming power of God's grace, active in everyday worship, devotion, and obedience towards God. Trinitarian themes undergirded this movement. Where Puritan influence was strong, preachers, catechisms, and Christian writers emphasized the work of Christ—and especially his death on the cross—in accomplishing human salvation. Likewise, sermons and popular writings called attention to the work of the Holy Spirit in leading Christians toward holiness in attitude and conduct, and taught that Christian prayer is to be addressed to God the Father, through God the Son, in God the Holy Spirit.

Beginning in the early eighteenth century, a movement called Pietism began to flourish in continental Europe. It emphasized the love of God and the personal experience of salvation through "religious affections." Much of Pietism embraced the trinitarian pattern of God's saving work in its practical and holistic (including emotional) implications for Christian faith and community. One influential pietist leader, Nikolaus von Zinzendorf (1700–1760), discussed the Trinity in thoroughly communal terms. He used the image of a divine family: Father, Mother (Spirit), and child (Son). However, his experientially rooted speculations did not always reflect adequate awareness of the crucial theological concerns that lay behind more traditional formulations.[2] In the Methodist movement, which began to flourish in America and England in the mid-eighteenth century, John and Charles Wesley frequently articulated Christian belief and God's saving and transforming work in believers' lives in sermons, occasional writing, and popular hymns that were overtly trinitarian.

### Reason, Experience, and Divine Transcendence

*From the doctrine of the Trinity, taken literally, nothing whatsoever can be gained for practical purposes, even if one believes one comprehends it—and even less if one recognizes that it surpasses all our concepts.*
                                                     Immanuel Kant, c. 1793[3]

In this same period, philosophers deeply influenced by the Judeo-Christian tradition—but disillusioned with Christian orthodoxy—began to intentionally detach the Western idea of God from the biblical and traditional sources that had originally led the early Christians to confess God as triune. Emerging Unitarianism held that the doctrine of the Trinity is a misrepresentation of biblical and early church teachings about God. Generic Theism regarded belief in one God as philosophically reasonable, but often conceived of God apart from the New Testament and orthodox trinitarian conceptions. The term *Deism* describes various influential seventeenth- and eighteenth-century forms of religious philosophy that reflected a general skepticism about divine revelation, the historical reliability of biblical accounts, traditional Christian beliefs including the doctrine of the Trinity, miracles, and what came to be called "the supernatural." In this view, the Deity had created the world, but is utterly *transcendent* and so is above and beyond active intervention in its continuing history.

---

[2] See Peter Zimmerling, "Zinzendorfs Trinitätslehre: Eine Herausforderung und Bereicherung in systematisch-theologischen Überlegungen der Gegenwart," *Evangelische Theologie* 51, no. 3 (1991): 224–45.

[3] Immanuel Kant, *Der Streit der Fakultäten,* 1, Anhang, 2, in *Immanuel Kants Werke,* vol. 7, ed. B. Kellerman, Ernst Cassirer (Berlin: Bruno Cassirer, 1922), 349.

As the Enlightenment flourished throughout the eighteenth century, various German thinkers sympathetic with religious faith attempted to make it intellectually plausible again through a variety of approaches. In these efforts, the orthodox doctrine of the Trinity did not fare well. Immanuel Kant (1724–1804) placed particular emphasis on reestablishing the moral foundations that religion had once provided for human society. He argued that all genuine knowledge must be established either through rational demonstration or sense experience. Since God's existence cannot be established in either of these ways, Kant reasoned that genuine knowledge of God was not possible. However, belief in God and in life after death are justified as practical assumptions because they are the basis of our confidence that living according to the moral law leads to ultimate happiness. But Kant's hypothetical God was little more than an idea, having almost nothing in common with the trinitarian God of Christian tradition. His explicit marginalization of the doctrine of the Trinity exercised a huge influence over Western thought after him.

Friedrich Schleiermacher (1768–1834) was a distinguished Christian pastor and theologian influenced by Pietism. In the early nineteenth century, he sought to make Christianity credible again to those "cultured despisers" who believed it was untenable on rational or practical grounds. Religion, he argued, is not primarily to be located in the realm of reason or moral action, but rather in the realm of feeling. It is "the consciousness of being absolutely dependent, or, which is the same thing, of being in relation with God."[4] Schleiermacher worked out this hypothesis in an elaborate and creative interpretation of Christian faith that has exercised enormous influence over Western theology ever since. His dominant concern was the relationship of God with human beings through Jesus Christ's redemption. The doctrine of the Trinity was placed as the conclusion to his entire theology. To the extent that this belief expresses and reflects "the union of the Divine Essence with human nature, both in the personality of Christ

---

[4] Friedrich Schleiermacher, *The Christian Faith*, ed. H. R. Mackintosh and J. Stewart (Edinburgh: T. & T. Clark, 1989), 12.

and in the common Spirit of the Church," Schleiermacher affirmed it as "the coping-stone of Christian doctrine." However, he went on to express grave reservations about the traditional creedal formulations, asserting that they affirmed "an eternal distinction in the Supreme Being" and that they eternalized, "in separation, the being of God in itself, and the being of God which makes union with human nature possible."[5] Because of his massive theological influence, Schleiermacher's sharply stated reservations about traditional trinitarian understandings of God further contributed to their marginalization in mainstream nineteenth-century academic theology.

In response to the growing skepticism of rationalists and biblical critics, Kant had sought to preserve at least the idea of God because he believed it was the necessary foundation for morality. Schleiermacher effectively insulated Christian faith from its intellectual critics, both biblical and philosophical, by locating it in the realm of feeling. In contrast, G. W. F. Hegel (1770–1831) tried to provide theology with a new foundation in philosophy through an all-encompassing abstract explanation of world process that saw all reality as the unfolding of the trinitarian idea.[6] Hegel's philosophical use of the concept of the Trinity was intended to correspond only formally to orthodox Christian belief in the Trinity. He saw statements of Christian doctrine as symbolic ways of depicting higher and more profound ideas. What the Trinity points us to is that God is an eternal process in which the divine is continuously and necessarily expressed in divine revelation, and in God's work in history. On all levels of thought and reality, a universal dialectical pattern of trinitarian process expresses itself in the constant triadic interplay of thesis and antithesis, leading to synthesis. For Hegel, this pattern became a key to explaining human knowledge, history, society, and culture.

In the wake of the Enlightenment, German philosophy and theology had tended to swing between two extremes. Both carried unfortunate implications for everyday Christian faith. Where

---

[5] Schleiermacher, *The Christian Faith*, 738–42.
[6] See, for example, G. W. F. Hegel, *The Philosophy of Religion*, trans. E. B. Speirs and J. B. Sanderson (London, 1895), 3:25.

God's transcendence (exaltedness above and beyond created reality) was emphasized, the possibility of any genuine, dependable knowledge of God was typically undermined. Such an utterly ineffable God often seemed remote, inaccessible, and uncaring. The other extreme was to see God as so involved with—or even tied to—world processes (often called divine *immanence*) that God's sovereignty as Creator over the created world was compromised. Such an immanent God often seemed impotent and unable to help Christian believers in their need. Although Hegel's use of the Trinity pushed the boundaries of Christian orthodoxy, it was influential in stimulating fresh trinitarian reflection on this problem among later thinkers more committed to traditional Christian formulations. Isaak August Dorner (1809–1884) developed with considerable insight the idea that belief in the Trinity enables Christian faith to appropriately acknowledge both God's transcendence and God's immanence. As the eternal and almighty Father, God is indeed utterly above and beyond all human comprehension and created reality. But in Jesus Christ, God has come near to human beings, entering our history. As the Holy Spirit, God governs, moves, and sustains the created world and lives in the church and within human beings. Thus, trinitarian faith enables Christians to affirm both divine transcendence and divine immanence. In the Trinity, Christians can embrace both of these poles of divine reality together without theological contradiction.[7]

## God Made Known in Self-Revelation

*The statement . . . that God reveals Himself as the Lord . . . we call the root of the doctrine of the Trinity.*
Karl Barth, 1932[8]

In the face of Modernism's relentless advance, especially in Germany, theology had often politely retreated, seeking to make

[7] See Isaak August Dorner, *System of Christian Doctrine,* trans. A. Cave and J. S. Banks (Edinburgh: T. & T. Clark, 1932).

[8] *Church Dogmatics,* vol. 1, trans. G. Bromiley (Edinburgh: T. & T. Clark, 1975), 1:307.

the best of its losses in order to retain academic credibility. However, the aggressive German militarism of World War I was firmly supported by its major theologians. In light of Germany's subsequent defeat, this apparent evidence of misplaced loyalty caused many to question the theological developments of Modernity and to seek a new footing for theology.

Karl Barth (1886–1968) was among the boldest proponents of a "new" starting point for theology. In 1932, with the first volume of his *Church Dogmatics*, he found this in the doctrine of the Trinity. For Barth, the doctrine of the Trinity was at the center of Christian teaching:

> The doctrine of the Trinity is what basically distinguishes the Christian doctrine of God as Christian, and therefore what already distinguishes the Christian concept of revelation as Christian, in contrast to all other possible doctrines of God or concepts of revelation.[9]

Barth saw in the doctrine of the Trinity the authentically Christian response to the relentless question of Modernity, "How can God be known?" The root of the doctrine of the Trinity is that God is self-revealing. In Jesus Christ, God the Father makes the divine nature known in time and space, within the parameters of human history and experience. By the Holy Spirit, God even opens us up to receive that knowledge. So Enlightenment attacks on the possibility of knowing God—which so many felt had been decisive—were actually overcome by the reality of God's own trinitarian self-revelation within human history and experience. Genuine knowledge of God does not depend on a human quest. Instead, in self-revelation God is Revealer (Father), Revelation (Son), and Revealedness (Holy Spirit).[10]

Barth developed his understanding of the unity and distinction within the Trinity from this starting point in revelation. Since God reveals the divine nature equally as Father, Son, and Holy Spirit,

---

[9] Ibid, 301.
[10] Ibid., 295.

these three are "the one, single, and equal God. The subject of revelation attested in the Bible, no matter what may be His being, speech, and action, is the one Lord."[11] Standing firmly in the Western tradition, Barth carefully disassociates the idea of three divine persons from any Modern connotation of "personality." This, he says, would constitute the worst kind of tritheism. There is only one divine "I."[12]

Among Barth's many profound contributions to contemporary trinitarian theology, another that cannot be overlooked is the way his ideas bridged the chasm previous theology had often supposed between who God is and what God does; between the *being* and the *activity* of God. Barth saw danger in this distinction. He championed the conviction that God revealed in Jesus Christ through the Holy Spirit is nothing less than or different from God's own self. If this were not the case, Barth pointed out, we would have no assurance that the God Christians worship is the true God. "The reality of God which encounters us in His revelation is His reality in all the depths of eternity."[13]

This point was stated still more forcefully by the German Roman Catholic theologian Karl Rahner (1904–1984). Rahner embraced and amplified Barth's idea that in the Trinity, God communicates God's own self to human beings. He pointed out that even though most Christian believers intend to be orthodox in their confession of the Trinity, practically speaking they are often "almost mere monotheists" in the actual patterns of their thinking, worship, and practice as Christians. "We must admit that, should the doctrine of the Trinity have to be dropped as false, the major part of religious literature could well remain virtually unchanged."[14]

Rahner suggests that this is due to the tendency of many Modern theologians—a tendency already noted in the historical survey above—to develop their whole idea and understanding of

[11] Ibid., 381.
[12] Ibid., 351.
[13] Ibid., 479.
[14] Karl Rahner, *The Trinity*, trans. J. Donceel (New York: Herder & Herder, 1970), 10–11.

God and God's characteristics before and without reference to the trinitarian persons. By the time the discussion turns to the Trinity, some theologians have already discussed everything really crucial about their concept of God.

Early twentieth-century theologians had inherited a strong emphasis on divine transcendence from the nineteenth century. As a result, they sometimes spoke about the Trinity from two different standpoints. The term *immanent Trinity* was used to indicate the Father, Son, and Holy Spirit as they are within God's own inner self or life. This was an effort to refer to who God is. The term *economic Trinity* had been used for God as Father, Son, and Holy Spirit at work beyond or outside the divine self in the world: creating, revealing, saving, relating, and acting on behalf of human beings. This was an effort to speak of what God does, and of God's relationship to the world and humanity.

The alternative, which Rahner proposed in continuity with Barth, is to insist that what God does in the world and in relationship to human beings as Father, Son, and Holy Spirit corresponds fully with who God is in God's own self. He stated this point in the axiom, "The 'economic' Trinity is the 'immanent' Trinity and the 'immanent' Trinity is the 'economic' Trinity."[15] Rahner's motive in making this statement was to return trinitarian faith to its basis in the biblical narrative of the gospel, so that it is no longer isolated from human salvation, Christian worship, and Christian living.

Nothing in God's inner nature could be inconsistent with God's self-revelation as Father, Son, and Holy Spirit in creation and human experience. If it were, revelation would be a sham, even deceptive. It would not be God's own revelation of self. There could be no genuine knowledge of God. The economic Trinity must, then, correspond with the immanent Trinity.

These basic trinitarian insights of Barth and Rahner have been developed further by the contemporary Scottish theologian Thomas F. Torrance (b. 1913). What we can know of the Trinity

---

[15] Ibid., 21.

in God's inner relations, we must learn from the activity of the Father, Son, and Holy Spirit in relationship to human beings in space and time. In pursuing this and other themes, Torrance has shown special concern in recent years for establishing common ground between the more Western trinitarian ideas of Calvin, Barth, and Rahner, and the trinitarian approach of the Eastern Orthodox tradition. He has been a major figure in recent Reformed-Orthodox dialogues, which have begun by pursuing consensus on the trinitarian heart of Christian faith.[16]

## "Divine Society" or "Divine Communion"?

*It would be unthinkable to speak of the 'one God' before speaking of the God who is 'communion,' that is to say, of the Holy Trinity.*

John Zizioulas, 1985[17]

Beginning in the late nineteenth century, socialism rose to prominence on the world scene. Various English and American theologians drawn to social (in contrast to individualistic) understandings of human nature began to elaborate what has since become known as the "social theory of the Trinity." Among the most articulate of these were Wilfred Richmond in England and Francis J. Hall in the United States, both of whom wrote in the first decade of the twentieth century. In this view, "personality" does not exist in isolation. It is defined through our relationships with others. The social trinitarians suggested that Father, Son, and Holy Spirit should each be deliberately associated with individual personalities in the Modern sense of the term. Richmond argued that "when Christian theology conceives God as a personal being, it does not conceive God as *a* person. Personality

---

[16] See Thomas F. Torrance, *The Christian Doctrine of God: One Being, Three Persons* (Edinburgh: T. & T. Clark, 1996); *Trinitarian Perspectives: Toward Doctrinal Agreement* (Edinburgh: T. & T. Clark, 1994).

[17] *Being in Communion: Studies in Personhood and the Church* (Crestwood, N.Y.: St. Vladimir's Seminary Press, 1985), 17.

attaches to God not as one Person, but as Three."[18] The Trinity should then be thought of as a "divine society." If God were a single personal being, the social trinitarians suggested, then God would be relationally dependent on the world. But if God is tripersonal, then God's personal self-existence is maintained in the interrelationships between the divine persons.

In this same period, an ancient and venerable tradition of trinitarian theology that had long been ignored and misunderstood in the West—that of Eastern Orthodoxy—began to receive fresh attention. Political developments in Eastern Bloc nations led to the emigration of some of the most articulate Orthodox theologians of the mid-twentieth century to the West. These theologians began to write in Western European languages, and this led to an extremely fruitful and long-neglected cross-fertilization between Eastern and Western theology, especially on the subject of the Trinity.

The work of Russian theologian Vladimir Lossky (1903–1958) was especially influential. His book, *The Mystical Theology of the Eastern Church*, was originally published in French in 1944, and was specifically intended to explain Eastern Orthodox beliefs to those in Western ecumenical circles. Lossky's approach to the Trinity drew upon the centuries of independent interpretation of early church ideas that derived from Eastern Orthodoxy's inheritance of Byzantine theological traditions. In particular, the Cappadocian explanation of the Trinity had remained authoritative throughout the history of Eastern Orthodoxy, whereas Augustine's influence had been resisted over the centuries.

The Eastern tendency to begin with the three persons—Father, Son, and Spirit—and to account for their unity through the idea of *perichoresis* was reflected in Lossky's approach. He regarded

---

[18] Wilfred Richmond, *An Essay on Personality* (London: Edward Arnold, 1900) II, 17. In the 1940s, various British theologians revived these ideas: C. C. J. Webb, *God and Personality* (London: George Allen & Unwin, 1918); Leonard Hodgson, *The Doctrine of the Trinity* (London: Nisbet & Co., 1943); Charles Lowry, *The Trinity and Christian Devotion* (New York: Harper & Brothers, 1946). Cf. Claude Welch, *The Trinity in Contemporary Theology* (London: SCM Press, 1953), 133–51.

it as the particular genius of the Cappadocians' contribution that they had taken what had previously been regarded as two synonyms and made use of them "to distinguish in God that which is common—ousia, substance, or essence—from that which is particular—*hypostasis* or person." Lossky was willing to associate the Greek idea of *hypostasis* with the modern idea of "person." Indeed, he believed the idea of "person" ("that *personal* quality which makes every human being unique") was a distinct contribution of Christian theology to human understanding.

However, Lossky was quick to point out (in a certain tension with Western "social trinitarian" ideas of "tripersonality") that the Three have "but one nature, have but a single will, a single power, a single operation."[19]

The contemporary Eastern Orthodox theologian John Zizioulas (b. 1931) begins here, with Lossky's suggestion that the idea of *person* is a unique contribution of early Christian theology to the history of ideas. For Zizioulas, the genius of the early Christian understanding of *person* that emerged in trinitarian discussion is that it means *being* has no meaning apart from persons. Neither God's existence nor God's identity—who God is—can be considered apart from the three divine persons. Threefold personhood is precisely the way God is God. And because God's identity consists in the relationship or communion of the three persons, human identity—as the divine image—also consists in the relationship or communion of persons.[20] According to Zizioulas, this insight emerged from the eucharistic experience of the early church, and guided the early church teachers into a radical new understanding of who God is: "the being of God is a relational being: without the concept of communion it would not be possible to speak of the being of God."[21]

Social trinitarianism and contemporary Eastern Orthodox trinitarian ideas share certain important themes in common. But

---

[19] Vladimir Lossky, *The Mystical Theology of the Eastern Church* (London: James Clarke & Co., 1957), 53.

[20] John Zizioulas, *Being as Communion* (Crestwood, N.Y.: St. Vladimir's Seminary Press, 1985), 39ff.

[21] Ibid., 16–17.

it is important to notice their different terminology and the opposite direction of their arguments, which reveals distinct motivating
concerns. First, social trinitarians often speak of God as a "divine
society" or "divine community." This idea almost inevitably suggests three Gods. In contrast, the Orthodox view of the Trinity is
usually more restrained. It speaks of the "communion" of the
three divine persons as constituting the unity of the one divine
being, thus avoiding any compromise concerning God's oneness.

*No* [margin annotation]

Second, the logic of social trinitarianism sometimes seems to
begin with human insights gained in social theory, and then to
argue to the way God exists as Trinity. There is an obvious danger
here. It would be little more than idolatry to project an understanding onto God primarily because it coheres with a contemporary
intellectual trend like socialism, or with concern for a particular
social agenda. In contrast, Eastern Orthodox trinitarian ideas derive
from an ancient and historic trajectory of biblical and theological
interpretation that stands outside—and thus may facilitate independent critique—of inherited Western explanations of the Trinity.
Eastern Orthodoxy argues from the unique insights of scripture and
early trinitarian theology to a radically alternative understanding of
personhood in community. On this basis, its perspective offers a
traditionally and historically rooted source for independent theological alternatives to individualistic, autonomous Western understandings of God, and of human identity and personality.

## God, Suffering, and Justice

*The triune God, who realizes the kingdom of his glory in*
*a history of creation, liberation, and glorification, wants*
*human freedom, justifies human freedom and unceas-*
*ingly makes men and women free for freedom.*
                              Jürgen Moltmann, 1981[22]

In the late nineteenth century, a variety of Jewish, British, and
Spanish thinkers attempted to reconceive traditional understand-

---

[22] *The Trinity and the Kingdom* (San Francisco: Harper & Row, 1981), 218.

ings of God's relationship to human suffering. Beginning in the early church under the influence of Greek philosophy, a dominant tradition in Christian theology had taught God's *impassibility*. This was the idea that in order to be divine, God must somehow be beyond or above all movement, diversity, passion, suffering, and feeling. Although this idea had been periodically challenged throughout the history of the church on biblical grounds, it remained an influential way of trying to guard divine sovereignty and transcendence. The horrors of World War II and the Holocaust gave additional urgency to the challenge of formulating a new understanding of God's relationship to human suffering. The need for this reevaluation was especially felt in Europe. There, a culture that many had regarded as the highest expression of human intellectual and cultural achievement in history had imploded, seemingly abruptly, into the epitome of human atrocity, victimization, and evil. Following the war, many were consumed by the question, "Where is God when humans suffer?"

In the period following World War II, Swiss Roman Catholic theologian Hans Urs von Balthasar (1905–1988) articulated a trinitarian theology that reflects deeply on this question. His insights were derived from the Hebraic traditions of the Old Testament and the defining Christian narrative of Jesus' life, death, and resurrection. Balthasar argued that the very being of God must be understood—from all eternity—in terms of dynamic, relational love: the self-sacrificial love dramatically demonstrated to us in the suffering and death of the divine Son, Jesus Christ, in his passion. These events authentically reveal God's heart. For Balthasar, through Jesus' suffering of genuine God-forsakenness on the cross, God takes human suffering into the divine life itself. And this is not just an event in created space and time, profound as that historic event was and is. The suffering divine love revealed through the Holy Spirit in the passion of the divine Son, Jesus Christ, reflects prior self-sacrificial, suffering love in the eternal divine relationships of Father, Son, and Spirit.[23]

---

[23] Cf. *The von Balthasar Reader*, ed. M. Kehl and W. Löser (Edinburgh: T. & T. Clark, 1982), esp. 153–54, 179–80.

In the 1970s, German Reformed theologian Jürgen Moltmann (b. 1926) drew new attention to the idea that suffering is a crucial aspect of God's inner-trinitarian relationships in his book, *The Crucified God*.[24] There, he argued that in the Son's suffering on the cross, the Father suffered compassionately through the Spirit. From its Latin root, *compassion* literally means "suffering with." To Moltmann, it is both legitimate and necessary to say and believe that God suffers in this trinitarian sense, and that God is a suffering God. He regards any idea of God that removed God from human suffering as not only unfaithful to the central message of the cross, but also helpless to show that God matters in the face of the deepest and most profound human needs.

Another of Moltmann's prominent concerns is the connection between less-than-fully-trinitarian Western ideas of God and oppressive political, social, and cultural patterns. At this point, his approach has much in common with earlier social trinitarianism. He suspects Western ideas of God (with their monotheistic tendencies) of encouraging hierarchical patterns throughout Western society in the areas of political theory and government, gender relationships, and social and economic relationships. These hierarchical patterns, he believes, have undermined the biblical vision of the kingdom of God. Where divine rule is understood hierarchically, humans seek positions of superiority over one another and oppress one another. In contrast, divine rule is rightly understood as the self-sacrificial, self-giving rule of God's love, based on a relationally trinitarian understanding of God's own nature and God's relationship with the world and human beings. Moltmann's presentation of the Trinity is that of a community of three equally divine persons existing in the unity of *perichoresis*. This trinitarian God draws us into the divine life and mission, as the three persons act as one in history—through the church and through liberating movements that operate outside the church—with the purpose that the biblical vision of an egalitarian kingdom of love, justice, and peace might be fully realized.[25]

[24] Jürgen Moltmann, *The Crucified God*, tr. R. A. Wilson and J. Bowden (New York: Harper and Row, 1974).

[25] Jürgen Moltmann, *The Trinity and the Kingdom*, trans. Margaret Kohl (San Francisco: Harper & Row, 1981), 197.

These ideas are expanded and applied more fully by Brazilian theologian Leonardo Boff.[26] Boff is part of a movement called Liberation Theology, which emerged in the 1960s in response to the extreme economic disparity between rich and poor throughout Latin America. Liberation theology emphasizes the biblical themes of God's special concern to provide justice for those who are poor, excluded, and oppressed, and God's judgment on those who use religious legitimation in order to further exploit victims. Boff identifies overtly with social trinitarianism, freely using the language of "divine community." He develops a trinitarian understanding of God—the loving divine community of Father, Son, and Holy Spirit—as the basis for a new vision of human society. He does not intend to project a communitarian understanding onto God's being in order to legitimate a particular form of human social organization. Rather, God exists from all eternity in the threefold unity of *perichoresis*. This communal divine reality of shared love is intended by God to be the basis for human society and relationships. Faced with the inadequate alternative of liberal-capitalist versus "socialist" understandings of society, the communion of love that is the Trinity provides the poor and oppressed with an alternative vision of a just society, constituted by relationships of love and respect among equals.[27]

## Overturning Stereotypes of God's Gender

*No language about God will ever be fully adequate to the burning mystery which it signifies. But a more inclusive way of speaking can come about that bears the ancient wisdom with new justice.*

Elizabeth Johnson, 1994[28]

With the rise of contemporary feminism in the late 1960s came a heightened awareness of the role that religious language could

---

[26] Leonardo Boff, *The Trinity and Society*, trans. P. Burns (Maryknoll: Orbis Books, 1988).

[27] Ibid., 7.

[28] *She Who Is: The Mystery of God in Feminist Theological Discourse* (New York: Crossroad, 1994), 273.

play in legitimating and sustaining particular forms of social oppression especially related to gender. In 1973, Mary Daly forcefully stated an influential analysis of this problem in the aphorism, "If God is male, then the male is God."[29] Although the assumption of God's maleness had not typically been formally taught in mainstream church theology, it had often been tacitly assumed in church circles. This assumption had immense potential for legitimating the idea that maleness is inherently superior to femaleness, and thus for contributing to the oppression of women.

In response to this growing awareness, feminist theology arose in the 1970s and 1980s. At its core was the critical analysis of traditional religious language and the effort to change patterns of speech and thinking that might reinforce gender bias or gender-based discrimination against women at any level of church or society. Among major feminist theologians, Rosemary Radford Ruether was prominent.[30] More recently, "Womanist theology" has reflected some of the same emphases, but with a greater focus on how issues of class, race, and culture as well as gender impact our perceptions of God, and how we articulate and live Christian faith.

As a part of this project, alternatives to the biblical and traditional use of the male pronoun in referring to God were intentionally sought for use in both theological and liturgical contexts. Based on the assumption that the language of "Father" and "Son" in scripture, the baptismal formula, and the historic traditions of trinitarian theology identifies God with the male gender, efforts to replace this language with gender-neutral alternatives were also made.[31] The most common substitute formula for "Father, Son, and Holy Spirit" proposed and tried in the 1980s was "Creator, Redeemer, Sustainer." Unfortunately, this alternative substi-

---

[29] Mary Daly, *Beyond God the Father* (Boston: Beacon Press, 1972), 19.

[30] See her *Sexism and God-Talk: Toward a Feminist Theology* (Boston: Beacon Press, 1983).

[31] See Ruth C. Duck, *Gender and the Name of God: The Trinitarian Baptismal Formula* (New York: Pilgrim Press, 1991), who explores a broad range of alternative combinations of terms.

tuted roles or activities shared by all three persons in relationship to creation for discrete names indicating their eternal distinction. As its modalist implications were recognized, other alternatives were tried. The challenge of finding different words that might retain even a significant portion of the traditional meanings proved daunting. "Creator, Christ, Holy Ghost" conveniently fit the meter of many traditional hymns, but it awkwardly confused various levels of trinitarian language. It identified the first person of the Trinity by means of a divine activity shared by all three persons, the second by means of the Greek translation of the messianic title that pertains to the salvation history of Israel, and the third with a linguistically antiquated but biblical and traditional trinitarian name. Recently, various trinitarian analogies proposed in the early church have been explored for their potential in providing liturgical substitutes for the traditional terms.[32]

A more thoroughgoing approach involved the attempt to reconceptualize the doctrine of the Trinity in female imagery that faithfully reflected the intentions and meanings of the traditional trinitarian terminology derived from scripture. Roman Catholic theologian Elizabeth Johnson has pursued this possibility with impressive sensitivity to the core truths of traditional trinitarian theology in *She Who Is: The Mystery of God in Feminist Theological Discourse*. Adopting the goal of "women's flourishing" as a guiding principle, Johnson begins with the assumption that all human language, including biblical language, applies to God symbolically. In particular, terms reflecting male gender ought not to be normatively privileged just because they are used in scripture in particular contexts, in particular ways, or by particular persons, including Jesus. Because of its feminine connotations in various biblical and traditional contexts, Johnson chooses the biblical concept of personified wisdom (Greek: *sophia;* as, for example, it is used early in the book of Proverbs) as an integrating idea for the Trinity. She then develops her understanding of

---

[32] For one example, see David Cunningham, *These Three Are One* (Oxford: Basil Blackwell Publisher, 1998), who recommends and uses Tertullian's analogy of source, wellspring, and living water as a substitute for Father, Son, and Holy Spirit.

the three persons in God as Spirit-Sophia, Jesus-Sophia, Mother-Sophia, one living God—*SHE WHO IS*. "*SHE WHO IS*" is Johnson's female rendering of God's self-revelation and concealment in the meeting with Moses at the burning bush (Ex. 3:14). If, with the tradition, we acknowledge that God is not male, we should have no reason to object if female images are substituted for male images. In using this terminology, Johnson intentionally opens the door to a different way of thinking about the relationship between God and the world as a "real relationship." She believes that when God is conceived in female images, it helps us to see "God in the world" and "the world in God" in a way that reflects more accurately the *perichoresis* of the divine persons among themselves; a *perichoresis* in which God also shares the divine life with the world and human beings.

## Trinitarian Faith without Patriarchy

Recently, a number of other Roman Catholic theologians deeply sympathetic with feminist concerns have incorporated elements of the feminist analysis of religious language into fresh discussions of the Trinity. These discussions retain essential continuity with traditional trinitarian faith, even as they reject the patriarchal assumptions that much of that tradition has communicated throughout the history of the church. Among these studies are Mary Ann Fatula's *The Triune God of Christian Faith* and Anne Hunt's *What Are They Saying About the Trinity?* Fatula provides a deeply devotional discussion of the Trinity as "God's intimacy with us" and as "the infinite vulnerability of a God who would disclose in trust and love for us the very secret of the divine life."[33] Her writing draws richly on biblical, historical, and contemporary examples of feminine imagery for God, even as it affirms the indispensability of traditional trinitarian language. Hunt provides an insightful survey of recent discussions of the Trinity that emphasizes its implications for liberation of the oppressed, for

---

[33] Mary Ann Fatula, *The Triune God of Christian Faith* (Collegeville, Minn.: Liturgical Press, 1990), 12.

feminist concerns, for the environment, for human suffering, and for the establishment of mutual, loving relationships between God and human beings, and between human beings and one another.[34]

In *God for Us: The Trinity and Christian Life*, Catherine Mowry LaCugna provides a fresh critical interpretation of the entire history of trinitarian faith. She critiques the increasing tendency in the history of trinitarian reflection to begin on the basis of an abstract understanding of God. Instead, trinitarian faith is rooted in God's saving purpose. This is "the comprehensive plan of God reaching from creation to consummation, in which God and all creatures are destined to exist together in the mystery of love and communion."[35] LaCugna sees a "rupture" between trinitarian teaching and "the economy of salvation" that reached its extreme in the high medieval trinitarian thought of Thomas Aquinas in the West, and Gregory Palamas in the East. She suggests that a major reason the Trinity became less and less central to Christian belief was that it was difficult to see what it had to do with everyday Christian faith, worship, and living. Graphically, she calls this "the defeat of the doctrine of the Trinity." This is because these approaches misrepresented the fundamental intention of Trinitarian belief. The Trinity is intended to tell the whole story of God and God's relationship with human beings. It faithfully describes who God is and what God does.[36] For LaCugna, it is inaccurate and unhelpful to even try to conceive of God apart from God's relationship to the world and human beings. Whatever knowledge of God and whatever access to God we might have is only within that relationship.

This guiding principle has important ramifications for Christian worship and life, which LaCugna sketches. She affirms John Zizioulas's insights: "the doctrine of the Trinity emerged in the assertion that God is *essentially relational*."[37] Based on what God

---

[34] Anne Hunt, *What Are They Saying About the Trinity?* (New York: Paulist Press, 1998).

[35] Catherine Mowry LaCugna, *God for Us: The Trinity and Christian Life* (San Francisco: HarperSanFrancisco, 1992), 223.

[36] Ibid., 209, 211.

[37] Ibid., 289.

has revealed to us about the divine *perichoresis* and the missions of the Trinity, persons are persons precisely in their relationships—first and decisively with God, but also with others—not as solitary individuals. Based on the Trinity, "personhood requires the balance of self-love and self-gift."[38] In response to the concerns raised by feminism and Latin American Liberation Theology, she embraces a trinitarian vision of "a human community structured by relationships of equality and mutuality rather than hierarchy," arguing that this can be "a true icon of God's relational life."[39] Reflecting the divine reality of the Trinity, freedom consists in being free for others. Our purpose is living in communion, or right-relationship, with the triune God, and with others in and through the triune God.

> God moves toward us so that we may move toward each other and thereby toward God. The way God comes to us is also our way to God and to each other: through Jesus Christ by the power of the Holy Spirit. This is our faith, confessed in creed and celebrated in the sacraments.[40]

Trinitarian theology issues in *doxology*, a word that refers to direct prayer and praise of God's glory. As we offer our prayers and praise to God the Father, through God the Son, in God the Holy Spirit, our theology and our experience of God's salvation are one. We direct our worship to the trinitarian God, who gives us glimpses of who God is in what God does, in revealing and saving and consummating the divine purpose for humanity and all creation.

[38] Ibid., 290.
[39] Ibid., 274.
[40] Ibid, 377.

# 5

# The Trinity in Christian Faith, Worship, and Life

*W*hen it comes to being a Christian on a day to day basis, everything turns on whether the God we believe in, worship, and serve is the Father, Son, and Holy Spirit of the New Testament and the triune God of the Christian tradition. It is the strong name of the Trinity into which we are baptized. It is in this God alone that we can confidently place our trust. It is this God alone whom we must worship and serve. Our belief in the Trinity is what makes possible the Christian conviction that in Jesus Christ, through the Holy Spirit, *God is for us.*

## Not Just Arithmetic

*The disregard of [the liturgical season of Trinity] may be due to the difficulty of harmonizing a reasonable faith with what appears to be an irrational doctrine, the doctrine of the Trinity.*

William Phipps[1]

When Christians talk about the Trinity, sometimes the unfortunate impression is left that the major issue at stake is a dilemma of arithmetic. How can one be three? How can three be one? Thomas Jefferson, it is said, became a Unitarian because he believed the doctrine of the Trinity was mathematical nonsense. Much of the project of developing

---

[1] "The Triune God," *Presbyterians Today* 84, no. 4 (May 1994): 20. This article was also a source for the following paragraph, although it provided no documentation.

analogies for the Trinity has focused around the issue of how three can be one. With this concern in mind, Augustine spoke of the root, the trunk, and the branches of a tree as all being—not three woods—but one wood. Many contemporary parents have tried to help their young children gain a sense of how God can be both one and three with a similar natural analogy like steam, water, and ice; each is distinct, and yet each is the same identical substance that bears the chemical formula $H_2O$. Children often resonate with the analogy of a hair braid. A single substance, parted into three sections, nevertheless intertwines as a single braid.

The issue of arithmetic captures particular attention where Christianity interacts or dialogs with the closely related religions of Judaism and Islam. These latter faith traditions view the trinitarian faith of Christians as a denial of God's unique oneness, and thus as the idolatrous worship of additional gods beside Yahweh. This same failure to get beyond the arithmetic has often been equally evident within Christian faith, worship, and life as well. The beloved Christian hymn "Holy, Holy, Holy, Lord God Almighty" is a moving expression of praise to the triune God. But if we are to begin to appreciate the profound implications of the Trinity for Christian faith, worship, and life, our praise must move beyond the perception that the significance of trinitarian faith is exhausted with the confession of "God in three persons." So what practical difference does the Trinity make for us?

### The Way We Know God

*In sharp contrast with every other religion, Christianity stands for the fact that in Jesus Christ God has communicated to us his Word and has imparted to us his Spirit, so that we may really know him as he is in himself.*

Thomas F. Torrance[2]

Deep within each one of us is a longing to know God. Not just any god. Certainly not a god of our creation, an imagined being

[2] *The Christian Doctrine of God: One Being, Three Persons* (Edinburgh: T. & T. Clark, 1996), 3.

that projects our own hopes and dreams, or the values of our culture, onto a giant screen. We yearn to know the true God. Yahweh. The One who is. The Creator of heaven and earth. The One who made everything, seen and unseen. The One who made *us*. In the strong name of the Trinity resides our confidence that the God of the Bible and historic Christian faith—the God of our baptism—is God indeed. In the strong name of the Trinity resides our certainty that this God's existence does not hang on our ability to prove it. In the strong name of the Trinity resides our assurance that knowing this God does not depend on the earnestness of our own searching, or on the tangible evidence we do or do not see around us, or on whether or not we have explored every possible religious option.

Philosophers and theologians since the Enlightenment have helped us to see the genuine limits of our human knowledge. Some have suggested there is such a deep chasm between human beings and God that human reason simply cannot cross it. In one sense, they are correct. God *is* so exalted and mysterious—so infinitely above and beyond our human categories and powers of reasoning—that no human speculation, logic, or intuition could possibly provide any reliable confidence that we know and are known by the true God. That is why our only knowledge of God is and must be in and through the Trinity. The Trinity, as we have learned from Karl Barth and others, means that the path across the chasm goes the other way. Not from us to God, but instead from God to us. Our minds simply cannot reach up to heaven. But they do not have to. In the Trinity, God has reached down to earth. The triune God has come into our world in Jesus Christ, making the divine nature known in time and space, on our human terms. The triune God has entered our lives in the Holy Spirit, opening our hearts and minds to recognize who God is. As Trinity, God has made known to us God's own self. The God whom we know in Jesus Christ by the Holy Spirit is the true God.

From the human side, we come to know God through faith. Many Christians have the impression that faith is what *we* contribute as human beings to knowing God. God makes the divine nature known; then it is our job to muster up enough faith to believe what God reveals. But listen to the way John Calvin talks about faith:

> Now we shall possess a right definition of faith if we call it a sure and certain knowledge of God's benevolence toward us, founded upon the truth of the freely given promise of Christ, both revealed to our minds and sealed upon our hearts by the Holy Spirit.[3]

Faith is trinitarian through and through. It is not something we produce ourselves, in an essentially human response to what God has revealed. Like revelation, faith is God's work, not ours. The same triune God who makes the divine nature known also awakens, focuses, and sustains faith in us. As the work of the Holy Spirit, faith is a divinely given receptivity to what the triune God shows us of God's own self. Faith is what results in us as the Holy Spirit instills the conviction that God's freely given promise in Christ is true. Faith is awakened from beyond itself by the triune God. It focuses beyond itself on the triune God. And it is sustained beyond itself, by the triune God. It is a firm and certain knowledge of God's goodness towards us. It is God's gracious gift.

### God Is Love

*The God who is triune communion of love does not need us in order to have someone to love. And for this reason, we are, each of us, really, unconditionally and freely loved.*

Mary Ann Fatula[4]

"What else do we want, each one of us, except to love and be loved?" With this question, Dorothy Day summed up another longing of our hearts.[5] As persons, we all have an inner need to

---

[3] John Calvin, 1559 *Institutes* 3.2.7.
[4] *The Triune God of Christian Faith* (Collegeville, Minn.: Liturgical Press, 1990), 24.
[5] *By Little and By Little: The Selected Writings of Dorothy Day*, ed. Robert Ellsburg (New York: Alfred A. Knopf, 1983), 213.

be in relationship. It is God who declares at the creation, "It is not good that the man should be alone" (Gen. 2:18). The image of God in which we are created does not encompass just a single gender: it is both female and male. Our very creation establishes God's intention that we live in relationship.

Human love takes many forms. It can be based on family ties, or on the desire to complete oneself in another, or on the sharing of mutual interests and concerns.[6] But for Christians, "God is love, and those who abide in love abide in God, and God abides in them" (1 John 4:16). The love Christians know and experience in God is a qualitatively different love. It is the unconditional, self-sacrificial love that is poured into our hearts by God the Holy Spirit; the same love that is exemplified and demonstrated for us once for all in the death and resurrection of God the Son. After Jesus' death and resurrection, the early Christians felt compelled to transpose the obscure Greek word *agape* into a specialized term that referred specifically to this unique love, conveyed by the Holy Spirit and expressed definitively in God's inestimable gift of God's own self in Jesus Christ. *Agape* is self-giving love. It is love that seeks the good of the other, no matter what sacrifice this requires of the giver.

> God's love was revealed among us in this way: God sent his only Son into the world so that we might live through him. In this is love: not that we loved God, but that he loved us, and sent his Son to be the atoning sacrifice for our sins. (1 John 4:10)

When Christians say "God is love," we are speaking of the Trinity. We have seen the profound way Augustine expressed this in the fifth century, when he suggested that we think of the Trinity as Lover (Father), Beloved (Son), and Love itself (Spirit). In the Middle Ages, Richard of St. Victor tried to explain why God is triune by appealing to the self-giving character of mutual

---

[6] C. S. Lewis has explored these concerns with great insight in *The Four Loves* (New York: Harcourt, Brace, Jovanovich, 1960).

divine love. This self-giving love, he suggested, needs a divine "other" with which love is shared, and a third in which it bears fruit, and which ensures that the divine love is not exclusive or possessive. More recently, Mary Ann Fatula has articulated this point concisely: "God is triune by being living relationships of love."[7]

God is *agape* love. This love is the giving of self to another. But love that arises from obligation cannot be free. And love that is not free is not love at its most profound. This is the importance of the Trinity for our appreciation of the love of God. God's own life of love is complete in itself, as the eternal, mutual sharing of love between Father, Son, and Holy Spirit. Since God is this Trinity of love, God's love for us can be a free choice—a completely unobligated gift of grace.

## God Is Gracious

*God is gracious to us—this is what the Confession of the Father, Son and Holy Spirit, says.*

Karl Barth[8]

Ultimately, our need and desire to love and to be loved can only be fulfilled from within the context of an intimate and secure love-relationship with God. But we know in our own experience how prone we are to turn away from God. We know our tendency to alienate ourselves from God and others, to live so that self-sufficiency protects us from the vulnerability of dependence. The risks of a love-relationship with God drive us to seek reassurance that this relationship would not depend on anything we could ever do or fail to do. We need to know that our own inadequacies cannot destroy this most important relationship.

One of the key commitments of the Protestant Reformation of the sixteenth century was that human salvation is "by grace alone, through faith." Grace is the biblical word for a free gift that is

---

[7] Fatula, *Triune God of Christian Faith*, 22.

[8] *Dogmatics in Outline*, trans. G. T. Thomson (London: SCM Press, 1949), 16.

completely undeserved and unearned. God's free gift to us is God's own unconditional, covenant love. A covenant is a solemn agreement, secure because its guarantee is God's own faithfulness. God's covenant love is firm and unshakeable. From the beginning of scripture, God has covenanted with God's chosen: "I will be your God, and you will be my people." When Jesus fulfilled the Old Testament messianic expectation, the security of that covenant relationship was opened up to include us, as we place our trust in him.

Now that Christ has come, God's grace is expressed, above all, in the freely given, unearned salvation that God the Father has extended to us in him, through the Holy Spirit. Ephesians 2:8–9 sum up the New Testament teaching about grace: "For by grace you have been saved through faith, and this is not your own doing; it is the gift of God—not the result of works, so that no one may boast." Because our relationship with God depends on God's grace alone, it is secure.

Ultimately, it is the Trinity that is the ground and source of God's grace. Because God exists eternally in three persons—a divine community of love—the self-giving of the divine life freely overflows in the sending of the Son and the Spirit into the world "for us and for our salvation," according to God's gracious will. Through the Holy Spirit, God the Father has given us God's own self in the free, undeserved gift of Jesus Christ. Similarly, through Jesus Christ, God the Father has given us God's own self in the free, undeserved gift of the Holy Spirit. John Calvin summed up the trinitarian work of God's grace in our lives:

> Grace is itself the power and action of the Spirit: through grace God the Father, in the Son, accomplishes whatever good there is; through grace he justifies, sanctifies, and cleanses us, calls and draws us to himself, that we may attain salvation.[9]

---

[9] John Calvin, *Institution of the Christian Religion* (1536), trans. F. L. Battles (Atlanta: John Knox Press, 1975), 2.20.

The Trinity is the source of our confidence that God is gracious toward us. This is the firmest possible basis of confidence. We can be sure that our own failings, sin, and inadequacies can never separate us from God. It is God's trinitarian grace, and not anything we could ever do or fail to do, that enables and secures this primary relationship.

## God Is Our Salvation

*The truth concerning the Triune God comes to humankind by the history of redemption, containing as it does the promise of salvation.*

Geoffrey Wainwright[10]

The biblical story identifies at least two obstacles that stand between us and the intimate, transparent, trusting love-relationship with the eternal God for which we long. The first is our sin. *Sin is the traditional word for all the ways we fall short of the purpose for which God created us.* It literally refers to "missing the mark" of God's intention for us. It describes the "chain reaction of selfishness" that characterizes our human condition.[11] Sin expresses itself in our stubborn self-centeredness. It is evident in our moral failings and our refusal and inability to live according to God's purposes revealed for us in scripture. It can be seen in our insistence on trying to pull everything off on our own; in our attempts to prove that we do not need God or anyone else. It is manifest in the hurt we cause ourselves and others.

When sin dominates our lives, we have turned our backs on God and God's purpose for us. This causes a breach in the relationship with God that God intends for us. In the guilt and shame that result, we can no longer meet God's gaze. We avoid the intimate, face-to-face relationship for which God created us.

---

[10] "The Doctrine of the Trinity: Where the Church Stands or Falls," *Interpretation* 45, no. 2 (April 1991): 126.

[11] Fatula, *Triune God of Christian Faith*, 43.

The second obstacle that stands between us and the eternal God's intended relationship with us is our mortality: the tendency towards corruption, decay, and death that resides within us all. God is eternal. We are not. Eternal life in the intimacy of God's presence is incompatible with the corruption that is part of our human condition. According to the Bible, this second obstacle also stands in direct opposition to God's created intention for us. It is a consequence of the first obstacle: human sin. In Paul's letter to the Romans, we are taught that "the wages of sin is death" (Rom. 6:23).

This is where the biblical idea of salvation comes in. Salvation addresses our need to be in right relationship with God. Equally, it addresses our need to grow toward the wholeness that enables us to faithfully reflect God in such a way that God's original, created purpose for us is fulfilled.

The New Testament dramatically introduces us to God's chosen way for overcoming both of these obstacles. It joyfully announces how we can be restored to the intimate, face-to-face, divine-human relationship for which we were created. Through the Trinity, the relationship is restored and consummated—not by anything that we do but by what God has done for us once and for all in Christ, and continues to do in and among us through the Holy Spirit. The trinitarian pattern of this wondrous way that God freely established for us—completely apart from any human deserving—is discernable in the biblical texts that tell us of our salvation. Romans 5:1–10 spells out this pattern with particular clarity. "While we still were sinners," the apostle Paul declares, "Christ died for us." We have been justified (put right with God) by Christ's freely shed blood. We have been reconciled to (restored to right relationship with) God through the death of God's own Son. We are saved through his life. So we have peace with God. Because of God's gracious salvation for us, we now have access to stand boldly in God's presence without guilt, shame, or fear. This confidence enables us to rejoice in our hope of sharing God's glory, because God's love has been poured into our hearts by the Holy Spirit that God has given us.

In gracious, self-sacrificial love, the triune God takes all the responsibility for restoring us to the intimate divine-human relationship for which we are intended. This enables us to fulfill the divine purpose for our lives. God does not leave us alone to find a way to deal with our own sin. Instead, like the Father in the parable of the lost son (Luke 15:11–32), the triune God rushes out to meet us, concerned only that our relationship might be restored. Rather than remaining aloof in righteous judgment, God has come onto our terms, seeking us out in the midst of our lostness.

Our salvation is trinitarian from beginning to end, as Athanasius pointed out with such clarity in the early church. It depends entirely on the confidence that in Christ's victory over sin and death, we have to do with God's very own self. Likewise, it depends on the conviction that in the transforming work of the Holy Spirit within us, we also have to do with God's very own self. Through Christ's life, death, and resurrection, God has assumed and restored our fallen human nature in order to save us both from our sin, and from the corruption and death that were its unavoidable consequences. Equally, through the Holy Spirit's ongoing work in the church and in human hearts and lives, God takes up residence today in our midst, transforming us toward the fulfillment of the divine purpose for us.

The contemporary worship song from Isaiah 12:2 expresses it in a nutshell: "Surely it is *God* who saves me." In the Trinity, God *is* our salvation.

## God Frees Us to Be Changed

*"Trinity" is the normative Christian model for understanding who God is; but who God is can never be separated from who we are now and who we are to become.*
Catherine Mowry LaCugna[12]

The Christian hope that God can change us into the people we are intended to be is rooted in the Trinity. In seminary, I became

---

[12] "The Practical Trinity," *Christian Century* 109, no. 22 (July 15–22, 1992): 679.

acquainted with an African man who exemplified this radical, transforming power. As a teenager, a military coup had erupted across his country. His father had been an official in the ousted government. My friend was playing quietly by himself in back of his family home when a military unit came to the home, set it on fire, and murdered his parents and siblings. He could only watch helplessly in terror. The cruel face of the unit commander was forever etched in his memory. The wounds from this traumatic experience led to deep pain and resentment as he moved into adulthood. Many times, he imagined himself seeking out his family's murderer, and exacting revenge by killing him with his own hands.

Years later, my friend became a Christian. In a country where many people were arbitrarily incarcerated simply for being associated with the wrong political regime, his African congregation took seriously the biblical injunction to visit and pray for prisoners. One day, as he entered a cell, he was confronted by the unforgettable face of the same unit commander he had watched preside over the execution of his family. All the pain and trauma of that terrible childhood experience flooded over him. This was the opportunity for revenge he had so often longed for. The urge to strangle the man on the spot almost overwhelmed him. But he closed his eyes and called upon God. As he did, the cruel visage that had haunted him for so many years was gradually transformed. In its place, he saw the gracious, compassionate visage of his Lord Jesus Christ, agonizing on the cross not only because of the man's complicity in his family's murder, but also because of his own enslaving pain and resentment. Moved by a gracious power beyond his own, he took the man's hand, prayed with him for God's blessing on his life, and went on to the next cell, forever freed and changed.

We all bear our own wounds and scars. These may come from hurts inflicted on our families from outside. But for those who live in post-Christian, politically stable Western cultures, they are just as likely to come from patterns of addiction, abuse, or deception within our families, or even within our own lives. Whatever their origin, they can trap, dehumanize, and immobilize us.

If we have any hope at all for the future, we long for the power to change. But even our most strenuous efforts are rarely sufficient. Instead, we find ourselves reenacting the very dysfunctions of which we have been victims. New Testament baptismal texts such as Colossians 2:8–3:17 remind us that baptism in the strong name of the Trinity initiates a lifelong process of liberation and transformation from the destructive forces that seek to hold us captive. A central portion of that text assures us that through baptism, we are partakers in Christ's own death and resurrection. Through the cross and empty tomb, Christ set aside the record of our own sin that stood against us with its legal demands, nailing it to the cross. At the same time, "he disarmed the principalities and powers and made a public example of them, triumphing over them in it" (Col. 2:11–15, author's translation).

The phrase "principalities and powers" in Paul's writings refers to whatever suprahuman forces around us threaten to overwhelm us and enslave us. These forces may be psychological, social, cultural, political, or spiritual. But by the power of the Holy Spirit, Christ's victory on the cross has the power to set us free. The text continues to spell out the implications of our baptism. If we have been raised with Christ, we are to seek the things that are above, where Christ is, seated at the right hand of God. We have died, and our lives are hidden with Christ in God. We have God's promise that when Christ our life is revealed, we also will be revealed with him in glory (3:1–4).

Whenever genuine change does occur in us, it takes place through the Trinity. This is the way God extends to us the wonderful privilege of participating in the divine life. By the Holy Spirit, the Father graciously extends this life to us according to the pattern of human wholeness exemplified for us in the Son. It is a work of divine grace from its inception through its completion. We receive the transforming grace of God as the Spirit opens us up, redirecting our hearts in harmony with God's purpose for humanity, embodied in Christ's own example. Colossians goes on to declare that in baptism, we have clothed ourselves "with the new self, which is being renewed in knowledge according to the image of its creator" (3:10). The goal is that on a human level we would become more and more faithful reflections of God in God's own triune life.

When we seek to be changed by the triune God, certain crucial dynamics that further this participation are involved. The discipline of prayer is primary. Whether prayer takes place in corporate worship or in solitude, it is essentially a communal discipline. We pray with and according to the faith of the whole community of Christ across the ages. We have seen that the divine oneness is expressed in a complete unity of will among the Persons of the Trinity. Our most faithful prayers seek and reflect this divine unity of will. Such prayer involves asking God to align our wills with the one divine will. The goal is that we will come to want what God wants. We pray that our desires would resonate with the mutually united desire of the Trinity. We long for our hearts to be synchronized with the beat of God's own heart. The Lord's Prayer expresses this in the petition, "Thy kingdom come, thy will be done, on earth as it is in heaven."

Accountability to other Christians within the community of faith is also a crucial dynamic through which God works to change us. This too is a reflection of the trinitarian life of God. The Father, Son, and Holy Spirit do not operate on their own in the *perichoresis* of the divine life. They operate mutually as one, sharing and amplifying the divine love that seeks the good of the other. In chapter 1, we saw that the Christian identity we receive in baptism resides in our relatedness to God and to one another. In practical terms, this means personal change occurs insofar as we are willing to be guided, supported, corrected, encouraged, and held accountable to God's purposes for us by others in the community of faith. In the Christian life, this will take tangible form in disciplines such as corporate worship, intentional Christian friendship, spiritual direction, small groups, or twelve-step groups.

As we grow in prayer, and as we live together as God's people in relationships of mutuality and accountability, it is the triune God who accomplishes change in us by the power of the Holy Spirit. Where the Spirit of the Lord is, there also is freedom from the powers of destruction that threaten to overwhelm, victimize, and enslave us (2 Cor. 3:17). God's almighty power is the ultimate authority in the universe. This power comes to focus in the Holy Spirit's transforming activity in the world. In this Spirit, the baptized are gradually conformed to the image of human wholeness that the Father has placed before us in the divine Son Jesus Christ. And in some small measure, we pray and hope that by the Holy Spirit, we may reflect the mutuality and unity that characterize the triune life of God.

## God Suffers with Us

*Because Jesus freely has entered into our human sin and suffering and made it God's own, our pain does not reveal that God has abandoned us but rather that the triune God is* with *us absolutely and without condition.*

Mary Ann Fatula[13]

The good purpose of the triune God for human life is gradual growth—in the Spirit—toward the wholeness we see in Jesus Christ, our pattern. But neither our world, nor our relationships, nor even our own lives easily yield themselves to this purpose. Tragically, a huge proportion of our human experience in this world falls far short of God's intention. Of course, more of our suffering than many of us would like to admit is at least partially self-inflicted. Much suffering is also caused by the wounds and pain that we inadvertently, or willingly, or perhaps even viciously inflict on others. But that leaves a whole range of conditions, circumstances, and phenomena that seem to fly in the face of the Christian claim that a good and loving God is moving creation and human history towards an ultimately positive outcome.

At this point, trinitarian faith can help us to lift our gaze beyond the seeming contradictions and logical cul-de-sacs of Modern theological discussions about God and evil. Instead of trying valiantly to rationally justify an abstract and predominantly

---

[13] Fatula, *Triune God of Christian Faith*, 103.

causal concept of "God" as good and loving in the face of suffering and evil, trinitarian faith simply affirms that the triune God holds the world and human beings in the divine embrace.

Trinitarian faith allows us to step back from the question, "*Why* does God allow this suffering, or pain, or evil?" Is God's vantage point available to us? Should it be? Questions are inevitable, but when we are consumed with asking "why" in the midst of suffering, we may distance ourselves from our God when we most need divine comfort. Our line of questioning implies that God is connected to suffering as its cause: either actively as the one who inflicts it, or passively as the one who at the very least, ought to prevent it.

In contrast, trinitarian faith asks more humbly: "*Where* is God in this suffering, or pain, or evil?" When the question is asked like this, we can honor Jürgen Moltmann's sensitive comment that "God and suffering belong together, just as in this life the cry for God and the suffering experienced in pain belong together."[14]

When the question of suffering is transposed in this way, the answer is not only less elusive, but ultimately more comforting and strengthening. It is a trinitarian answer that takes its bearings from the poem of the Suffering Servant in Isaiah 53. In the suffering of the Servant Jesus Christ the Son on the cross, we have God's own assurance that in our suffering, God stands with us, not against us. In the Spirit, we are mysteriously united to Christ in his and in our own suffering. To use Moltmann's imagery, in the suffering of the divine Son on the cross, the Father suffered compassionately through the Spirit. In this sense, our suffering—and especially our willing and sacrificial suffering on behalf of others—can be a particularly faithful reflection of God's own being and work; a vital bridge of connection and empathy with the triune God of love, who suffers compassionately with us.

This is what we most need to know when we or a loved one suffers. Rational explanations, no matter how subtle, fail to address the various levels of our being in which pain is experienced

---

[14] *The Crucified God*, 49.

most profoundly: physical, psychological, and spiritual. The one thought that we could not bear in the midst of our suffering is the suggestion that the God of love—the One in whom we have placed our trust and for whom we have given our lives—stands over/against us, inflicting this suffering upon us. In the Trinity we find our confidence to the contrary. In tender compassion, our God has refused to remain aloof, choosing rather to "empty himself of all but love"[15] in order to enter into and absorb our suffering in its very depths, triumphing over it in the mystery and sovereignty of the divine life and wholeness. It is not we who were afflicted and abandoned by God. It was Christ on the cross. And in that miraculous and mysterious trinitarian event, infinite love freely created what we can only think of—with trembling hesitation—as an abyss or separation in the inner divine life. The gracious and loving will of God to save us requires the very life of the incarnate Son. The love of the Father and the Spirit for the Son is pitted against the love of the Father, Son, and Spirit for us. The only begotten Son—the second person of the Trinity—is "handed over" to suffering, alienation, emptiness, abandonment, and death. But it is an abyss of self-sacrificial, self-giving love, in which God reaches out to embrace us in our human suffering. And in this embrace, suffering, evil, and death are dealt the ultimate defeat that only divine love could deliver.

[15] Charles Wesley, "And Can It Be That I Should Gain" (1738), see *Hymns for the Living Church* (Carol Stream, Hope Publishing Co., 1977) Hymn 248.

6

# Trinitarian Communion
# and Human Communion

$A$s we step into the third millennium since Jesus, the great
crisis of Western culture may well be a crisis of relationship. Ironically, the computers and televisions that connect
us to one another around the globe have also led to a painful
new isolation. When we sit in front of a television or write
and read messages on a computer screen, we are exposed to
the images and ideas of real persons. We receive informa-
tion about and from real persons. But are we taking part in
real relationships? Or are we retreating from real relationships, into an artificial, humanly created and controlled
realm in which images and abstract ideas substitute for—
and eventually become identified with—persons? Given
what we have learned so far from our discussion of the
church's confession of the Trinity, what could it possibly
mean to be a "person," apart from real face-to-face relationships of intimacy, intercommunication, mutuality, and accountability?

Our immediate contemporary crisis of relationship has
deep roots in Western culture. The idea of a *person* as an individual center of consciousness and self-determination is
foundational to Western democratic traditions. Our ideas of
*freedom* reinforce this understanding, centering as they do
in the supposed freedom from any restriction or constraint
on our independence. Our culture teaches us to think of
freedom as freedom *from* others. As a result, we often view
receptivity to others as naivete, dependence on others as

failure, responsibility for others as burdensome, and vulnerability with others as weakness.

If we grew up during the Cold War, we were raised in an environment in which the glories of Western individualism were frequently extolled, and the evils of communism frequently enumerated. However, the more these earlier walls between West and East have crumbled, the less we are likely to regard this sharp opposition of alternatives as adequate. Instead, we may even view the relentless erosion and fragmentation of traditional Western social structures that we are experiencing—including those of nation, community, church, neighborhood, marriage, and family—as problems largely stemming from this individualistic legacy. With this new willingness to step back and critically evaluate our own received assumptions may come a new openness to alternative understandings of human personhood and human community.

How can we live and flourish together as human beings in real, interpersonal relationships with one another? In a world where the bonds between persons seem more and more difficult to sustain, what would it mean to be genuinely and fruitfully interconnected with one another in our families, friendships, marriages, neighborhoods, churches, communities, nations, and world? And what might the Trinity have to do with such a pervasive transformation of human life?

## Divine Communion

*Because God is personal and not impersonal, God exists as the mystery of persons in communion.*

Catherine Mowry LaCugna[1]

In chapters three and four, we have become familiar with two different trajectories of trinitarian faith, the Eastern and the Western. In different ways, both trajectories centered in the affirmation that *God is essentially relational.*[2] In the West, this was often

---

[1] "The Practical Trinity," *Christian Century* 109:22 (July 15–22, 1992), 681.
[2] The phrase comes from LaCugna, *God for Us*, 289.

expressed in the idea that in the divine being, the three divine persons of the New Testament—Father, Son, and Holy Spirit—have their distinct identities in their relationships with one another. Others in the West taught that God exists as the overflow of divine, self-giving love shared between the three equal divine persons. In the East, the language and imagery of *perichoresis*—of three distinct divine persons indwelling and inhabiting and existing in one another—more typically expressed this conviction that God is essentially relational. In this Eastern trajectory, the divine relationships constitute God's oneness. The mutuality of threefold personhood is precisely the way in which God is the one God. God's being exists in the intimate intercommunion of Father, Son, and Holy Spirit. Remember the Eastern image of the three divine persons seated around a table sharing a meal evocative of the Eucharist. This reflects the *koinonia*—the mutual indwelling—that characterizes God's own essentially relational existence.

### Creation, the Image of God, and Human Communion

*Since God is perfectly personal and relational, and since we are created in the image of God, then we will be most like God when we live out our personhood in a manner that conforms to who God is.*
Catherine Mowry LaCugna[3]

Throughout the biblical narrative, we are taught that we—as human beings—are created by this triune God in God's own image. If *God* is essentially relational—and not a solitary individual, conceived after the image of modern Western ideas of the human self—then it follows that the divine image consists in *our* interpersonal relatedness. God intends the divine *koinonia* to be reflected in human *koinonia*. We reflect God most authentically in relationships lived according to God's intention. The first chapter of Genesis is an important biblical source for these

---

[3] "The Practical Trinity," *Christian Century* 109:22 (July 15–22, 1992), 682.

connections. At the climax of the creation account, God says in verse 26, "Let us make humankind in our image, according to our likeness." The text continues, "So God created humankind in his image, in the image of God he created them; male and female he created them." The *koinonia* for which God created us has two dimensions: vertical and horizontal. The inseparability of these two dimensions is indicated in the New Testament in 1 John 1:3: "we declare to you what we have seen and heard so that you also may have *koinonia* with us; and truly our *koinonia* is with the Father and with his Son Jesus Christ." The vertical dimension is primary. That we are created as persons in the divine image means we are created for interpersonal relationship with the interpersonal God: the Trinity. Augustine's beautiful prayer expresses this truth. "You have made us for yourself, and our hearts are restless until they find their rest in you."[4] This thought is usually reflected directly in the wording of the Great Prayer of Thanksgiving that many Christians offer to God as we gather around the Lord's Table for the sacrament of Communion. From the Latin, *communion* literally means "union with." This name reflects the trinitarian reality of the sacrament: God the Spirit unites and reunites us with God the Father as we receive God the Son in his saving work. One formal Great Prayer of Thanksgiving expresses the trinitarian mystery of human communion with God in the phrase, "You formed us in your image, setting us in this world to love and serve you, and to live in peace with your whole creation."[5] In the gracious, intimate, love-relationship with God that the Holy Spirit opens up for us through Christ's incarnation, death, and resurrection, we reflect God most thoroughly and authentically.

In such prayers, we are reminded of the inseparability of the vertical and horizontal dimensions of *koinonia*. God did not create us as single, solitary human beings to be considered primarily as individuals. "It is not good that the man should be alone; I will make him a counterpart as his partner" (Gen. 2:18, my trans-

[4] Augustine, *Confessions* I.1.
[5] *Book of Common Worship* (Louisville: WJK, 1993), 69.

lation). A crucial reflection of God's own trinitarian, relational reality can be found in the biblical teaching that the divine image in humankind is to be found in the personal interrelatedness of our twofold creation as male and female. Male and female gender are two distinct yet inseparable *hypostaseis* of a single and common human nature. Each is indispensable and irreducible, and yet both are necessarily related. If we "are who we are" as we reflect the relational God, then the fact that we are created in the twofold distinction of male and female assumes and requires that we be human *in relationship* with other human beings. It also suggests that apart from interpersonal relationships, our humanity cannot be fully realized. Apart from relationship, we reflect God only inadequately.

We are created for relationship—communion—with God and one another. The relational, triune God made us to live in God's own self and to be together in community. This is what it means to reflect the triune God as human beings created in God's image.

## Trinitarian Communion in the Church

The primary context where we are invited and enabled to reflect God's own essential relationality is in the community of Christian faith, the church. But for many of us, church is not obviously or primarily an experience of deeply meaningful relationships of communion with others. What we call "churches" today can seem to be little more than buildings where organizational meetings are held and public speeches with a religious twist are made. This sort of church experience is not even a pale reflection of the relational, triune God's intention. Many who have left the institutional church over the past forty years have gone because they have become disillusioned in the face of this obvious discrepancy.

When our individual experiences of "church" fall short of God's created intention for human communion, we may be tempted to retreat into private religious experience. Millions of Americans who do not hesitate to affirm some form of Christian faith nevertheless actively or passively choose to spend Sunday mornings exercising, catching up on work, catching up on sleep, pursuing a hobby such as fishing or hunting, or cultivating a vague sense of divine transcendence in a place of natural beauty. This is even more true at the many other times throughout the week when nuts and bolts church ministries are being planned and carried out. Many others have intentionally left Christian faith for some other religious path that they can practice in private—a path that requires no communal or institutional affiliation, demands little sacrifice, and involves little accountability to others.

On the other hand, we may be tempted to substitute some other form of human community for the experience of communion that God intends for us in the church. In the 1950s in suburban churches in America, the cool formalism and social conformism that often characterized mainline churches led many to seek more authentic and intimate human community in the nuclear family. To this day, many American Christians continue to idealize the elusive experience of "family" as the primary unit of human community. Beginning in the 1960s, the resistance of many congregations to obviously needed social change led many young people to seek more authentic human community in mass protest movements, in various nontraditional communal living arrangements, or in promiscuous or serial sexual relationships. Adults who longed for more intimate interpersonal communion sought it in record numbers through leaving one partner or family with the hope of finding greater intimacy in another. The 1980s and '90s have witnessed the proliferation of a variety of recreational and self-help groups. These often function as inadequate substitutes for the more comprehensive vertical and horizontal *koinonia* that the triune God intends for us, and for which we have all been created. The communion that we hunger for—but seem unable to create for ourselves in our marriages, our families, or our friendships—we continue to seek in broader communal experiences that we hope will fill the loneliness and emptiness we feel.

What might a community that faithfully reflects God's intentions for human relationships look like? Paul suggests in the New Testament that it would look like a human body, constituted by its various parts and indistinguishable from them. Christ is the head of this body. First Corinthians 12 emphasizes that after Christ's physical ascension to the Father's presence, as Christians *we* are now the body of Christ on earth. We share God's life together in communion with one another. Individually, we are members of Christ's body. A *member* is literally a *limb*. It takes arms, legs, hands and feet for a body to be whole. This "membership" and the interdependence with one another that it assumes is the consequence of our baptism. In the same context, the apostle Paul can say, "In the one Spirit we were all baptized into one body . . . and we were all made to drink of one Spirit" (1 Cor. 12:13).

Within this one body, Christian believers reflect God's own triune relationality as we mutually serve one another in the church. We share with one another the love, grace, and strength we receive from the triune God. The diversity in unity that characterizes the Trinity is reflected on a human level. This is a unity because of—not in spite of—the diversity of backgrounds, cultures, races, priorities, generational groupings, and economic means within the Christian community. Together, distinct and diverse human persons comprise Christ's one body. Each represents a unique perspective and brings unique gifts of the Spirit. When we participate together in the life of the Spirit, sharing these gifts, the common good is served. The Father's sending of the Son and the Spirit into the world as the embodiment of God's own mission has its parallel in the sending of Christ's body, the church, into the world in the power of the Spirit. We reflect God outward. As we do, the world and its inhabitants are invited to share in the divine purpose for which they were created, by participating in God's own life through participation in the church.

In Acts, Luke uses the term *koinonia* to depict the shared life of the early church, just after the resurrection.

> They devoted themselves to the apostles' teaching and *koinonia* (living in accountability, mutual participation in one another's concerns, intimate interpersonal relationships), to the breaking of bread and the prayers. Awe came upon everyone,

because many wonders and signs were being done by the apostles. All who believed were together and had all things in common (Greek: *koinos*); they would sell their possessions and goods and distribute the proceeds to all, as any had need. Day by day, as they spent much time together in the temple, they broke bread at home and ate their food with glad and generous hearts, praising God and having the goodwill of all the people. And day by day the Lord added to their number those who were being saved. (Acts 2:42–47)

People outside the church identified the early Christians by the depth of their common life and by their mutual commitment to one another and to the common good. One early church writer observed that others typically said about them, "See how they love one another!"

It is helpful to consider examples of *koinonia* in the early church of nearly two thousand years ago. But it is more challenging to identify genuine *koinonia* in Christian gatherings and institutions today. What might *koinonia* look like if it were authentically expressed in our churches at the turn of the third millennium since Christ?

### Communion in Our Worship

*Christians worship God with whom they are in relationship. Liturgy itself is participation in the trinitarian* koinonia *through which the community of Christ is brought into "right relationship" with God, and its members with each other.*
Catherine Mowry LaCugna and Kilian McDonnell[6]

Because God exists in the eternal *koinonia* of Father, Son, and Holy Spirit, human *koinonia* begins in, depends on, and grows out of our living relationship with the triune God. This God extends to us the privileges of worship and prayer as primary

---

6 "Returning from 'The Far Country': Theses for a Contemporary Trinitarian Theology," *Scottish Journal of Theology* 41:2 (Spring, 1988), 197.

means by which that relationship is cultivated, maintained, and nourished.

It is common in our time for people to treat worship as if it were an entertainment event, in which personal taste is primary. Visitors to a worship service are prone to evaluate the music or the sermon as something to be "liked" or "disliked." After worship, we hear the comment, "I didn't get anything out of it." In an effort to connect with younger generations and those outside the church in a time of rapid cultural change, many congregations are adopting contemporary musical styles, and turning to more pragmatic and less traditional and theologically informed orders of worship. Other congregations focus on the importance of preserving classical Christian worship order and styles, and on passing down received Christian hymns and aesthetically profound music from prior generations. Inevitably, disagreements develop, and congregational conflict sometimes results. Contemporary commentators freely speak of "worship wars."

Christian worship is not primarily a matter of taste or style. It is certainly not primarily a matter of passively receiving, or of "getting something out of" what church leaders or paid professionals do for us. Neither is it primarily something that *we* do for God, as if in the work of worship, we were limited to our own human resources. It is certainly true that in authentic worship, worshipers are called by God to be profoundly active, as well as profoundly receptive. But at the most basic level, it is God's relationship with us, and our relationship with God, that is the primary concern of worship. That is why genuinely Christian worship is and must be trinitarian.

Christian worship is the communal event in which the church and its members are defined, restored, and renewed together in our primary relationship with the triune God. As we have seen, we are all created for *koinonia*: open, unhindered interpersonal communion with the interpersonal, triune God. At its best, Christian worship is where this relationship of communion between God and God's people is most authentically rooted, nourished, and brought to fruit. Such a relationship is possible only as God the Holy Spirit connects us to Christ; to all that God has done for us in the Son to restore us to right relationship with God through his life, death, resurrection, and ascension. In trinitarian worship, God the Father extends divine grace, love, goodness, comfort, presence, challenge, and motivation to us through God's Word and Spirit. We respond to God's initiative as God the Spirit opens our hearts to God's grace, presence, and ministry, placing before us again all that God has done for us in the Son.

On a human level, the event of worship is rich with prayers (said or sung together) that express praise, offer thanks, and seek God's forgiveness, comfort, healing, and strength. Worship centers in hearing and responding to the Word, read aloud in scripture and proclaimed in preaching. It is sealed in the celebration of baptism and the Eucharist. As a community and as individuals, we are moved to humble confession, jubilant praise, heartfelt thanksgiving, receptivity to God's leadership and guidance, awareness of our utter dependence on God, deeper faith and trust, and the offering of ourselves as God's servants and witnesses. Worship culminates in the sending of the people into the world.

On the divine level, the triune God is active in every aspect of worship. God bestows, shapes, and inspires our human capacities in such a way that in worship, God's dynamic activity actually *becomes* our genuinely human activity. The Spirit motivates and the Son mediates, as worship is offered to God the Father, through God the Son, in God the Spirit. God makes God's own self known to us in the Word, and present to us in the Spirit. We are actually loved, forgiven, and graced with God's real presence. The sending of the people into the world follows and carries through the pattern of God's own sending of the Son and the Spirit.

Trinitarian worship is not primarily something we offer to God. Rather, it is gracious participation in the triune God's own life and *koinonia*. This *koinonia* is the work of the Holy Spirit, who unites us to Christ in his unbroken communion with God the Father.

## Communion in our Prayer

*Baptismal and eucharistic invocation of the triune name, "Father, Son, and Holy Spirit," and prayer in the defining Christian pattern, to the Father with the Son in the Spirit, were the substance of the church's worshiping from the beginning.*

Robert Jenson[7]

As we learn about the Trinity, questions often arise about how God should be addressed in prayer. We pray according to the same trinitarian dynamic that undergirds, guides, and enlivens our worship. Following the pattern of Jesus' own prayers and the Lord's Prayer, the New Testament often speaks of God the Father as the one to whom our prayers are addressed (cf. Eph. 3:14–21). Jesus, the Son, has opened up the way of access for our prayers through his sacrificial offering of himself on the cross (cf. Heb. 4:14–16). God present in us as the Holy Spirit is the source of our prayers, and even of our desire to pray. Genuine communion with God and others in prayer is the work of the Holy Spirit, who interprets our needs and desires according to God's purposes for us, made known in the human nature of Jesus Christ:

> Likewise the Spirit helps us in our weakness; for we do not know how to pray as we ought, but that very Spirit intercedes with sighs too deep for words. And God, who searches the heart, knows what is the mind of the Spirit, because the Spirit intercedes for the saints according to the will of God. (Rom. 8:26–27)

That is why Christians have been taught since the early church to pray in God the Spirit, with or through God the Son, addressing our prayers to God the Father. The practice of addressing the "holy and blessed Trinity" directly in prayer was common in the late Middle Ages in the West. It was based on Augustine's idea that for Christians, the term *God* without further specification

---

[7] "Jesus in the Trinity," *Pro Ecclesia* 8:3 (Summer 1999), 310.

normally refers to the whole Trinity. However, the Protestant reformers expressed certain reservations about this practice, based on the fact that both the term *Trinity* and Augustine's ideas reflect later theological developments. The reformers emphasized that our prayer and worship of God should take place in the language and frame of reference of scripture.

In Western trinitarian traditions, with their concern to protect God's oneness, some have discouraged prayers addressed to the Son or to the Spirit. However, as we have seen, very early prayers addressed to Christ in Aramaic (the language Jesus most probably spoke) are found even in the New Testament (1 Cor. 16:22; Rev. 22:20). The prayer "Come, Holy Spirit!" also dates from the earliest centuries of the church. By the fourth century, Basil of Caesarea encouraged the church to pray "to God the Father, with the Son, together with the Holy Spirit." Not long afterward, the Ecumenical Council of Constantinople spoke of the Holy Spirit as One "who with the Father and the Son together is worshiped and glorified."

Direct address of the Son or the Holy Spirit has solid historical precedent, but it is not without risks. It presents the temptation (to which some worshiping communities often succumb) to artificially divide up the one work of the triune God by functions. For example, the Father might be praised for God's power, the Son might be sought for God's mercy, and the Spirit might be petitioned for God's comfort. There is a provisional sense in which scripture does associate particular aspects of the one divine work with particular persons of the Trinity. But we must keep in mind that all three divine persons are involved in all of God's work in the world, in the way appropriate to each. Otherwise we approach the precipice of modalism.

What about the practice of addressing prayers to God as "Mother?" This is now encouraged in certain mainline denominational settings as a recommended alternative to regular use of the name "Father" in both public and private prayer. In the first chapter, we have already affirmed the importance of Christian sensitivity to the need for reversing the destructive legacy of patriarchy. We have briefly considered the role that naming God as

"Father" may or may not have in contributing to that legacy. As we saw there, gender is an attribute of creation. The creator of gender is not subject to it. God is not male. Christian teachers can help believers realize this from our earliest opportunities to teach children how to pray.

Within this awareness, we may continue to joyfully cherish and gratefully speak the name "Father" in our prayers. "Father" was Jesus' own way of addressing God. "Father" is the way Jesus, our most reliable access to the knowledge of God, taught his followers to address God. "Father" is a way of addressing God that corresponds with the trinitarian language of our baptism, the creeds, and the entire Eastern and Western traditions of trinitarian faith—traditions that provide the primary resources for our Christian understanding of who God is and what God does.

But we must cherish and speak the name "Father" in constant awareness that God is "father" in a unique, divine way, a way that transcends all limited and flawed human parental images, male and female. Christians believe that by the Holy Spirit, scripture is the thoroughly reliable witness to God's self-revelation in Jesus Christ. Insofar as our address to God is faithful to the biblical witness, we can be confident that by that same Spirit, our prayers connect us with complete reliability to the true God and no other. But even biblical language is also necessarily human language. Human language can never capture, comprehend, or exhaust the reality of the divine life. So there is always a sense in which even biblical terms must be qualified in the way they apply to God. This recognition calls for concerted efforts in the church to disassociate God's unique and perfect fatherhood from the inevitably inadequate fathers and father-images that we have experienced in our own families. Such images have sometimes become deeply destructive or even demonic, filtered as they are through the imbedded and oppressive patriarchy of Western culture. To allow only the limited metaphors of our human experience and culture to provide the content for our ideas of divine fatherhood would be to flirt with idolatry. Instead, we must make the opposite and constant effort—with scripture— to allow our biblically revealed awareness and experience of

God's perfect, loving, gracious, even *motherly* fatherhood to provide the norm and pattern for all human fatherhood and the criterion for the Christian subversion of the destructive legacy of patriarchy.

Although the Old and New Testaments offer no examples of prayer addressed to God as "Mother," they do provide ample precedent for the use of maternal metaphors in referring to God. The biblical image of divine motherhood is an important and indispensable one for fully appreciating the richness of God's relationship with us. Psalm 131 offers the prayer, "But I have calmed and quieted my soul, like a child quieted at its mother's breast; like a child that is quieted is my soul" (v. 2, RSV). In Isaiah 49:15, God conveys the unshakeable stability of divine covenant love with this moving promise: "Can a woman forget her nursing child, or show no compassion for the child of her womb? Even these may forget, yet I will not forget you." In Isaiah 66:13, God vows with all the unconditional depths of motherly compassion, "As a mother comforts her child, so I will comfort you; you shall be comforted in Jerusalem." First Peter 2:2 encourages us to "long for the pure, spiritual milk" of the word of God, so that by it we "may grow into salvation—if indeed you have tasted that the Lord is good," thus likening God to a nursing mother. Calvin, in speaking of God's willingness to accommodate divine revelation to the level of our human capacity to receive it, pointed out that God is obliged to lisp in speaking to God's children, like a nurse lisps in speaking to an infant.[8] Julian of Norwich, who freely spoke of the second person of the Trinity as "God our Mother," was bold enough to pray to God as Mother in direct address, although she also cherished and freely addressed God using the biblical language of God's fatherhood. Based on the precedents outlined above, many others have followed her example—at least in their individual prayers—expressing the *koinonia* and

---

[8] Calvin, *Institutes*, I.13.1.

gender-inclusiveness of the universal Christian church throughout time and space. On the other hand, public prayers have most often remained within the parameters of the more reliable and trustworthy language that scripture explicitly uses for addressing God.

While not all may feel there is sufficient warrant in scripture and tradition for directly addressing God as "Mother" in prayer, all Christians who seek greater sensitivity to the way language shapes our perceptions (and sometimes contributes to gender oppression) can intentionally vary our address to God, using the wealth of feminine or gender-neutral terms available in scripture and Christian tradition. In Psalm 123, worshipers lift up their eyes to God, enthroned in the heavens, "as the eyes of a maid [look] to the hand of her mistress." In Matthew 23:37, in the depths of compassion, Jesus compares his own compassion for God's people to that of a hen who "gathers her brood under her wings."

Those who have learned a Western language other than English are well aware that it is an obvious mistake to equate linguistic gender in other languages with sexual gender. Still, it is interesting to note that the Hebrew word for "spirit" (*ruach*) has feminine linguistic gender. The New Testament term for "spirit," including the Holy Spirit, is linguistically neuter, not masculine. The Old Testament and New Testament terms for "wisdom" are linguistically feminine, and wisdom is personified in Proverbs as a woman (1:20–21; 3:13–18; 4:5–9; 8:1–9:12). Because wisdom is very closely associated in scripture with who God is and what God does (Prov. 3:19–20), diverse traditions of Christian prayer have often addressed God directly as Wisdom (sometimes using the Greek term for wisdom, *sophia*). In trinitarian terms, the idea of divine wisdom has usually been associated with the second, rather than with the first person of the Trinity. This is because the biblical characterizations of divine wisdom most resemble those of the divine Word as it is described, for example, in the first chapter of John's Gospel.

Terms that describe God's relationship with us are also frequently used in scripture and Christian traditions of worship and prayer as terms of direct divine address to God; terms such as creator, redeemer, judge, covenant-giver, shepherd, liberator, comforter, sovereign. Metaphorical terms drawn from God's creation and even human creation are also used to address God in scripture and Christian worship and prayer: rock, wellspring, fire, light, or fortress.

In contrast to the corporate nature of worship, you might be accustomed to thinking of prayer as a more personal kind of communion with God. Prayer is certainly deeply personal. But for Christians whose God is the Trinity, *personal* is not the equivalent of *individual,* and it is certainly not the opposite of *corporate.* Our identity as persons is in our relatedness. Because we are the body of Christ, all prayer is corporate (the Latin *corpus* is the word for "body") and interpersonal, whether we pray alone, with a friend, or in a large congregation. We are members of one another.

In fact, prayer is one of God's most wonderful and mysterious ways of linking us together as Christians. This is the "communion of saints," a phrase from the familiar Apostles' Creed of our baptism. It refers to all of God's people throughout history and around the world. In prayer, God the Spirit connects and unites us with the whole body of God the Son throughout time and space, everyone whom God the Father has called. In this trinitarian *koinonia* of prayer, the normal physical limitations that our createdness would ordinarily place on our ability to be in communion with one another are mysteriously transcended. As we pray, the Holy Spirit connects us interpersonally with other Christians of all times and places as members of Christ's one body. This is true whether they live in this world or in God's presence, and whether they are traveling, or going to school in another city, or suffering miles away in the hospital, or enduring persecution on the other side of the world. It is God's own interpersonal communion within the Trinity that is the basis, pattern, and dynamic of the communion we share with other believers through prayer.

## Communion in Our Life Together

*We are meant to know by experience the joy and strength of our communion with the triune God and with one another. . . . Wherever we go, we will not be alone and alienated but at home—home in the triune God, home in one another.*

Mary Ann Fatula[9]

The triune God's intention for communion with us is fulfilled when the worship and prayer of the church define, restore, and continually renew this most important relationship. Our vertical *koinonia* with God offers a clear alternative to the crisis of relationship that we are experiencing in contemporary Western culture. But God has also created us for *koinonia* in our horizontal relationships with one another in and through the church. What might this horizontal aspect of *koinonia* look like if it were authentically expressed in today's churches?

Throughout our culture, congregations are struggling to address the crisis of relationship that so many are experiencing. In our efforts to respond to the created human need to be connected with one another in relationship, we plan generationally defined groups for people of every life stage, from preschool children and youth through seniors. We organize singles groups to address the relationship needs of the unmarried and the previously married. We fill the week with church activities designed to strengthen human relationships: from potluck suppers to exercise programs, from dances to athletic teams, from game nights to small groups. But if we try to create the *koinonia* we seek by focusing horizontally on one another—by just "being together"—we will find that it is elusive. Whenever glimpses of genuine *koinonia* do surprise us in the life of our congregations, they grow naturally out of vertical *koinonia* with the triune God; *koinonia* that is grounded, established, and sustained in trinitarian worship and prayer. The human communion that God intends for us is only possible as the

---

[9] *The Triune God of Christian Faith*, 112.

overflow of God's own trinitarian life, manifested in the body of Christ by the Holy Spirit.

When trinitarian worship and prayer *are* the vital wellspring of a congregation's life, the community of faith begins to experience foretastes of the overflow of God's own interpersonal *koinonia.* Paul's depictions of "the body of Christ" are no longer just interesting metaphors to aid us in visualizing the life of the early church. Instead, they begin to function as actual descriptions of the interpersonal receptivity, interdependence, responsibility, and vulnerability that the congregation experiences every day in its life together.

> *Welcome one another, therefore, just as Christ has welcomed you, for the glory of God.*
>
> Romans 15:7

One of the first signs that God's own trinitarian *koinonia* has begun to overflow in the life of a congregation is a new attitude of receptivity to those who are not yet part of the church or the Christian way of life. In genuinely receptive relationships, long-time members are less concerned with our own needs, security, and social boundaries. We are more concerned to welcome those who have been outsiders. As Romans 15:7 suggests, our openness to others arises from our own awareness that Christ has welcomed us. Having been outsiders to God's mercy ourselves, we gratefully extend to others the lavish grace with which we ourselves have been welcomed. At full strength, this receptivity has no strings attached; it is extravagant. Like the father in the parable of the lost son (Luke 15:11–32), it willingly risks humiliation in order to welcome those in need of grace. It crosses societal boundaries of economic means, race, gender, generation, vocation, culture, background, and even viewpoint, in order to draw in those who have been "far off" (Eph. 2:13). How many congregations are eager to welcome a rehabilitated felon, along with his or her family? How often have we welcomed the homeless into our common life, or into our homes? Have we been so gripped by God's unconditional welcome that our churches can extend God's loving embrace to those in the grip of sexual addiction? It is one thing to provide services off-premises. That still keeps those who were "far off" at arm's length. It is quite another to welcome them as Christ has welcomed us. Earlier we noted that the unity of the Trinity is a mysterious unity that exists because of, not in spite of, divine diversity. Of course, this is not the way of the fallen world apart from God. If we do what comes naturally, we will follow the pattern of those around us, believing unity in the church requires uniformity. As a result, our churches will continue to be largely segregated by worship style, political party affiliation, economic means, race, culture, and theological viewpoint. But that has not been God's way among us. Jesus sought out the outcast, welcomed the stranger, and brought good news to the oppressed. At Pentecost, recorded in Acts 2, the Holy Spirit communicated the good news liberally, across the vast spectrum of human languages and cultures. As those who know that we are created in the image of God's own triune *koinonia*, Christian believers seek to reflect the divine unity through intentional diversity; a diversity that is as wide as our God's saving intention.

> *But God has so arranged the body . . . that . . . the members may have the same care for one another. If one member suffers, all suffer together with it; if one member is honored, all rejoice together with it.*
> 1 Corinthians 12:24–26

As we have seen, interdependence is another crucial aspect of the communion and work of the divine persons in the Trinity. In John 5:19–24, Jesus expresses the interdependence of the Father and the Son:

> The Son can do nothing on his own. . . . [W]hatever the Father does, the Son does likewise. . . . The Father judges no one but has given all judgment to the Son, so that all may honor the Son just as they honor the Father.

Later Christian teachers recognized that this divine interdependence also extended to the relationship of the Spirit to the Father.

and the Son. Gregory of Nyssa and Augustine set the precedent for all later trinitarian faith, teaching that every divine action in creation and human life is the concerted work of all three divine persons.

We may have been socialized to think of depending on others as a sign of personal failure or inadequacy. That impression grows out of our Western idea of "persons" as self-sufficient individuals who control their own destinies. But when the Trinity is the pattern for our human communion in the church, interdependence multiplies our ability to fulfill God's purposes. In *koinonia*, divine strength, creativity, imagination, and energy resonate and are amplified among us as each member of Christ's body shares what they can offer for the common good. A recent television special featured the hundreds of groups that have tried to conquer Mount Everest. Many of these groups seemed to have one thing in common. When they reached the highest, most dangerous parts of the peak, the groups tied themselves together with rope. They tackled the really difficult weather, cliffs, and crevasses together. They were inseparably bound together. Completely interdependent, they stood or fell together. And when one went forward, all went forward together.

There will be disappointments if we allow trust or expectations to be misplaced. The interdependence that characterizes trinitarian *koinonia* must not be mistaken for an immature dependence upon other human beings or institutions.

> But speaking the truth in love, we must grow up in every way into him who is the head, into Christ, from whom the whole body, joined and knit together by every ligament with which it is equipped, as each part is working properly, promotes the body's growth in building itself up in love. (Eph. 4:15–16)

Every church has its share of desperately needy people, seemingly unreceptive to the empowering comfort of God's Spirit, who instead merely drain the human resources of well-meaning human caregivers. This is not trinitarian interdependence. Dependence becomes an obstacle to Christian maturity when it does not ultimately strengthen each believer for deeper trust in the triune God and for the mutual ministry of giving and receiving that characterizes healthy interdependence. As we learn together to depend upon God's own dependability, expressed in and through one another, difficult choices will have to be prayerfully made between what others expect or demand of us, and what is really in accord with God's ultimate intention for their wholeness.

Interdependence cultivates, and in turn depends on, the closely related divine quality of compassion. Compassion is sharing in and—through the Spirit—mysteriously helping to bear the suffering of others: "Rejoice with those who rejoice, weep with those who weep" (Rom. 12:15). We have considered the way in which the triune God compassionately assumes, shares, and bears our suffering in the suffering and death of God the Son on the cross. When trinitarian *koinonia* characterizes a congregation, the community—as the body of Christ on earth—is mysteriously enabled by God to follow after the pattern of Jesus Christ the crucified God, assuming, sharing, and sometimes even bearing the suffering of the particular individuals of whom it is comprised. "If one member suffers, all suffer together with it; if one member is honored, all rejoice together with it."

> *Bear one another's burdens, and in this way you will fulfill the law of Christ.*
>
> Galatians 6:2

> *Let each of you look not to your own interests, but to the interests of others.*
>
> Philippians 2:4

Closely related to interdependence is the mutual acceptance of responsibility for one another. In much of our culture, we are encouraged to view responsibility for others as a burden. Disabled persons or aging parents who might once have been cared for by their own families are now often placed in institutions or nursing homes. Welfare "reform" is wildly popular on both sides of the political aisle, often motivated by the individualistic assumption that we are responsible only for ourselves and "our own." When our children become difficult to raise, many of us simply give up as parents, leaving the job to others in the name of "personal" freedom and fulfillment.

Responsibility for others *is* a burden. But we are created as persons in inseparable communion with one another. In the midst of these cultural tendencies, we who are called to live in the *koinonia* of the triune God are challenged to bear one another's burdens; to look not to our own interests but to the interests of others. In the *koinonia* that is the body of Christ, we are mutually responsible for one another. Our first concern is not for ourselves and "our own," but for others. This goes against all our natural instincts of self-preservation. It is truly evidence of God's trinitarian grace in our lives when we are given the strength to wake up early every Sunday in order to transport a shut-in member to worship. When we give birth to a child unexpectedly conceived, open our family life or home to someone who is alone, give hours each week balancing the church's finances, or expend our life savings as a volunteer in mission, we reflect the triune God in whose image we were created.

Life together in *koinonia* has equally radical implications for what our culture calls "*our* possessions" and "*our* money." The New Testament teaches we are stewards, not owners, of all that God places at our disposal. A Christian steward is one who administers property on behalf of Another. As a pastor of mine used to say, *koinonia* means "If I have a car, you have a car. If I have a computer, you have a computer. If I have a bank account, you have a bank account."

Responsibility *for* one another implies responsibility *to* one another. But in our culture, this kind of accountability is often identified with interference. There is a danger here. We are wise to be cautious toward those who expect us to be accountable to them when they refuse to be accountable to the triune God. A primary expression of our accountability to one another in the church is our joint accountability to the original biblical witness to God's self-revelation in Jesus Christ through the Holy Spirit. In Colossians 3:16, our responsibility to "teach and admonish one another in all wisdom" depends entirely on our willingness to "let the word of Christ dwell in [us] richly."

*Send letters to*
*Sodbury*
*is*
*July*

We all have to be accountable to things that are less than ulti-mate. Scripture assumes our provisional accountability to civil governments, employers, and parents, as long as this account-ability does not compromise our primary accountability to God, or our consequent accountability to one another in the church. But every human power, authority, and person is subordinate to our ultimate accountability to God and God's purpose for our lives. This includes civil authorities, the supposed authority of political parties and ideologies, the authority of our family tradi-tions, and the influence of our family members and friends. The accountability that grows out of *koinonia* is shared accountability for living together according to that divine purpose. It is as we live in this shared accountability to God's intention—the restora-tion of the divine image in every aspect of human life—that we most faithfully reflect God's own trinitarian communion.

> *It is the God who said, "Let light shine out of darkness," who has shone in our hearts to give the light of the knowledge of the glory of God in the face of Jesus Christ. But we have this treasure in [ordinary] clay jars, so that it may be made clear that this extraordinary power be-longs to God and does not come from us.*
> 2 Corinthians 4:6–7

One of the great temptations that our culture poses to *koinonia* is the temptation to regard what is called "personal privacy" as an inalienable right. In civil terms, such a right has certainly been upheld in our courts. But in the church, our instinct to guard our privacy, living unto ourselves, is diametrically opposed to our personhood. As persons created in the image of the triune God, we are essentially relational. Our reluctance to open up to others in our times of need has devastating consequences for the inter-personal communion that is God's created intention for us as human persons.

We have been taught that self-sufficiency, the ability to take care of ourselves without needing others, is a near-ultimate virtue. When our lives are falling apart, it is terrifying to seek support, prayer, and help from others, no matter how desperately we may need it. It is terrifying even to admit to others that we *have* needs. Vulnerability seems like weakness.

But as our lives become more deeply permeated with God's trinitarian grace, we are gradually set free to acknowledge the extent of our inability to handle things ourselves. Our sense of who we are is less and less dependent on whether we measure up to the standards of our background, our friends, our culture, or even our God. Instead, it becomes more and more deeply rooted in God's gracious, unconditional love for us. We are set free to share our shortcomings, our failings, and even our sins with others. As we share, we discover together that our needs are not so much weaknesses to be conquered, as they are the glue by which the Spirit binds us in one faith to the triune God and to one another. We know that whatever progress we may make towards becoming the people God intends us to be is *God's* work in us. We freely acknowledge that in ourselves, we are "[ordinary] clay jars, so that it may be made clear that this extraordinary power belongs to God and does not come from us." We seek to live in the glorious light of Jesus' humble example, who in his humanity depended completely on the presence and fullness of the Holy Spirit to be the person God intended him to be, and to do the work that God intended him to do.

When the Christian community conducts its common life in this vulnerable, transparent way, the Christian message can truly be embraced as good news by the wounded, discouraged, and defeated of the world. As we freely share our neediness and our inability with one another in *koinonia*, we model clearly in our own lives and in our interpersonal communion the fact that it is the God of grace, not anything that comes from us, that is the source of whatever strength, love, or goodness others may see in us. This is a wellspring of hope to the world in its alienation and pain. If the triune God can work in and through us, needy and hurting as we are, then others may dare to hope that perhaps the same God can also work in and through them too. In this way, the trinitarian vulnerability that our *koinonia* allows is translated into trinitarian evangelism.

# 7

# Sharing in the Triune God's Mission to the World

*T*he horizon of the church's communion with God and one another lies beyond itself in the world. Our brief glimpses of *koinonia* in the church point us toward God's ultimate, universal purpose: the participation of *all creation* in the *koinonia* of God's own trinitarian life. The vast scope of this divine intention is revealed in the images of the universal reign of God found throughout the scriptures. Old Testament prophets anticipated God's creation of a new heaven and a new earth (e.g., Isa. 65:17–25; 66:22–23). With Mary and Zechariah, Gospel writers and their congregations expected the Messiah to bring a new era of justice, mercy, salvation, and peace (Luke 1:46–55, 67–79). They knew God's reign had come upon them in the ministry and teaching of Jesus (Matt. 12:15–32; Luke 12:31–40; 13:18–30). The apostle Paul envisioned the whole creation set free from its bondage to decay, that it might "obtain the freedom of the glory of the children of God" (cf. Rom. 8:18–20). The seer of Revelation contemplated God's home among mortals, dwelling with all the redeemed. God's people would flourish in a transformed existence without tears, death, or pain (Rev. 21:1–4).

The gracious privilege of participating in the *koinonia* of God's trinitarian life cannot be possessed or kept by the church. Yahweh chose Israel to be a "light to the nations, that my salvation may reach to the end of the earth" (Isa. 49:6). At Jesus' birth, Simeon took the tiny baby in his

arms, "a light for revelation to the nations" (Luke 2:32). Just before Jesus went to the cross, he prayed that the loving *koinonia* he
shared with the Father might be extended to his disciples and all
those who would believe after them, so that the world would
know that the Father had sent him (John 17:22–23). After the resurrection, Jesus placed the disciples' mission in direct continuity
with his own: "As the Father has sent me, so I send you." Imme-
diately, he breathed on them, saying, "Receive the Holy Spirit"
(John 20:21–22). These biblical texts press for trinitarian articulation: God's own triune mission to the world provides the source,
pattern, and impetus for the church's mission to the world.

## God's Mission and Our Mission

> *The mission of God . . . is the participation of the Church
> in the Spirit's witness to what the Father is doing with the
> whole maze of events which make up human life—namely
> to sum up all things in Christ, in whom they were all
> created.*
>
> Lesslie Newbigin, 1963[1]

At the heart of the Christian message is the good news that
through the Trinity, *God's own story has taken and continues to
take tangible shape in human history.* The generous, mutually
self-giving life shared within the Trinity freely overflows. God
graciously wills to share the divine love, communion, life, and
beauty outside God's self. In an amazing act of divine vulnerability, God creates the world of time and space in and for
freedom—an expression of God's loving purpose for it. Human
beings are created in God's image, to live in communion with
God and each other. When those same human beings repudiate
God's created intention by turning our backs on God's gracious
care and guidance, the whole creation reflects and bears the consequences of that awful rejection. Its once-clear testimony to its
Creator is now ambiguous.

---

[1] *Trinitarian Faith and Today's Mission* (Richmond: John Knox Press, 1963), 50.

But this turning away of the creation cannot thwart God's gracious, loving purpose for the world. From all eternity, God has already determined that the eternal processions of the Son and the Spirit within God's own life would be extended in the sending forth (the missions) of the Son and the Spirit into the midst of the creation. In the mission of the Son, God enters our human situation, definitively expressing God's own self within the limits of created time and space. The eternal birth of the divine Son in the triune heart of God is "extended outside of God to us."[2] In the fullness of time, God's Son is born as a Jew in a manger in Bethlehem, for us and for our salvation. The embodiment of God's gracious self-giving, the Son, becomes human flesh and blood. In his baptism, he is anointed by the Spirit to redeem human history by fulfilling the messianic roles of priest, king, and prophet. In the Son's suffering and death on the cross, it is God who bears the awful consequences of human repudiation of the divine purpose. The biblical history of salvation dramatically climaxes in Jesus' resurrection from the dead. As risen and ascended *Messiah-Priest*, his sin-bearing death opens up our way back into the communion with God for which we were created. As risen and ascended *Messiah-King*, he rules, governs, and leads the church forward as its suffering Servant, transfiguring every merely human understanding of power and authority. As risen and ascended *Messiah-Prophet*, he definitively displays the Father to the world, drawing people toward explicit faith in himself by embodying the divine purpose for human life.

In the one, sovereign purpose of the triune God for the world, the mission of the Spirit parallels and extends the mission of the Son. The eternal breathing-forth of the Spirit within God's own trinitarian life is extended "outside of God to us" in the church's ongoing experience of Pentecost. All that the triune God has done for humanity in Jesus Christ now begins to be integrated into the continuing human story through God's own trinitarian action in the world. Through our baptism in the strong name of the Trinity,

---

[2] Mary Ann Fatula, *The Triune God of Christian Faith*, (Collegeville, Minn.: Liturgical Press, 1990), 69.

the Spirit unites God's people to the risen and ascended Christ in his messianic ministry as priest, king, and prophet for the world. In the Spirit, the church participates in Christ's *priestly* ministry for the world. Freely forgiven, we are called to freely extend God's gracious forgiveness and healing to all who suffer from the brokenness of sin in its various forms: social, political, environmental, relational, personal. In the same Spirit, the church participates in Christ's *royal* ministry in the world. Gripped by our own experience of the humble, self-sacrifical service of the crucified One, we are called to repudiate the false power and authority of physical, economic, political, or intellectual coercion, pouring out our own lives for the transformation of human institutions, communities, and individuals toward the wholeness that the triune God intends. Finally, in the Spirit, the church participates in Christ's *prophetic* ministry in the world. Having beheld the light of the knowledge of the glory of God shining in the face of Jesus Christ, we are called to proclaim the good news that God's gracious love for the world is offered to all in him.

In this way, the church's sending forth in mission is actually participation in the trinitarian mission of God as Son and Spirit, the mission in which God graciously invites the whole creation into the loving embrace of God's own trinitarian life. The Christian conviction of the Trinity becomes a kind of shorthand for the Christian gospel itself. Our mission as the church grows out of the good news that God's own story has taken and continues to take tangible shape in human history.

### Our Baptismal Calling

*Baptism is the practice of the doctrine of the Trinity, because it is through faith and baptism that the trinitarian history of God's kingdom takes possession of men and women.*

Jürgen Moltmann, 1981[3]

---

[3] *The Trinity and the Kingdom*, trans. Margaret Kohl (San Francisco: Harper & Row, 1981), 95.

Christian belief in the Trinity is ultimately about *God's* identity. Who is this God whom we know, worship, and serve? Why this God and not some other? The answer to that question is this: Our God is Yahweh: the One whose identity is definitively personal because it is established, revealed, and declared in divine words, commitments, and acts. Our God is Yahweh, the One who is always faithful to the divine promise. And as God's own story has taken and continues to take shape in human history, we can go on to say: Our God is Yahweh, the one who raised Jesus Christ from the dead in the power of the Holy Spirit.[4] Our God is the Father, Son, and Holy Spirit, into whose triune name we are baptized. Our God is the Father, Son, and Holy Spirit, who created us to participate in God's own trinitarian *koinonia*, and to live joyfully in that *koinonia* with one another in the church. Our God is the Father, Son, and Holy Spirit, whose gracious mission to the world overflows from the *koinonia* of God's own generous, mutual self-giving.

If trinitarian faith is about God's identity, then our shared baptism in the strong name of the Trinity is ultimately about *our* identity as God's people. That identity, that confidence of *who we are*, grows out of our conviction and experience of *Whose we are*. We are the baptized. Our triune God holds us firmly and securely in the divine embrace. We are the baptized. Our identity is constituted by our relationships with God and one another in the baptismal community, the church. We are the baptized. In life and in death, we belong—not to ourselves—but to the God who proved faithfulness in raising Jesus from the dead by the power of the Spirit.

Our baptism in the strong name of the Trinity is our confidence of our God, our identity, and our belonging. Our baptism is also our calling. Baptism calls us to embrace and participate in the triune God's own mission to the world. We are recalled to this mission when we vow to "guide and nurture . . . by word and deed, with love and prayer" each tiny baby, held up before us in hope

---

[4] Cf. Robert Jenson, *The Triune Identity: God According to the Gospel*, (Philadelphia: Fortress Press, 1982), 39–40.

as we respond to God's Word in worship. We are recalled to this mission each time a newly believing teenager or adult is drawn by the Spirit to a Christian congregation, to be joined in baptism to its life, worship, and ministry. And we are recalled to this mission whenever we remember and live out our own baptism, binding ourselves again and again to the strong name of the Trinity in which it was performed.

The strong name of the Trinity was first written in remembrance of Jesus' personal missionary call to his followers. There are no clearer words with which to articulate our baptismal calling.

> All authority in heaven and on earth has been given to me. Go therefore and make disciples of all nations, baptizing them in the name of the Father and of the Son and of the Holy Spirit, and teaching them to obey everything that I have commanded you. And remember, I am with you always, to the end of the age. (Matt. 28:18–20)

# Glossary

*All terms defined in the glossary are printed in italics each time they are used, to indicate ideas that may be further clarified by consulting another entry.*

*attribute*   A quality that human beings regard as characteristic of God. Divine *attributes* include qualities that are used to describe God in scripture, which may also describe humans in some sense, such as love, goodness, faithfulness, graciousness, mercy, wisdom, and kindness. Other *attributes* identified in theological speculation about God, and which ordinarily could not be applied to humans, include omniscience, omnipresence, *transcendence*, and *immanence.*

*being*   When used as a noun, the living *essence* of someone, especially God; the divine continuity to which *attributes* are attached; that which distinguishes God as God; the shared divine reality in which Father, Son, and Spirit are equally divine. See especially *ousia*; see also *substance, essence, reality.*

*begotten*   Generated or caused, with particular allusion to the male role in the reproductive act, and with emphasis on the similarity of *essence, being,* or nature between that which generates and that which is generated. The term *begotten* describes the specific manner in which the Son proceeds from the Father, in distinction from the *procession* of the Spirit. The term is typically used in deliberate contrast with "created" or "made," in which what is caused is of an unlike *essence* or nature to that which causes it. See also *generation, procession.*

coinherence
A term derived from Latin and often used to express the idea of *perichoresis* in Western theology.

communion
Literally, union with. (1) In describing believers' relationship with God, the literal meaning is primary. (2) In describing the relationships within the Trinity, the literal meaning of "union with" expands toward the idea of *perichoresis.* (3) When used to describe human relationships with other human beings, *communion* indicates a mutual participation in and sharing of one another's lives and concerns; an inseparable connection between persons. In its strongest horizontal sense, *communion* implies believers are actually constituted and defined in relationship to one another, after the divine *perichoresis* within the Trinity. See *koinonia.* (4) In Christian theology, *communion* is also a common word for the sacrament instituted by Christ at the Last Supper, in which by the Holy Spirit, believers are united with Christ and one another as bread and wine are received in faith as Christ's body and blood.

Deism
A view, prominent in the eighteenth century, that a remote and transcendent Deity created the world and set its processes in motion but does not normally intervene in its affairs.

dialectical
A method of thinking that begins with ideas viewed as opposite and works to reconcile them in a meaningful resolution that helps refine both concepts in terms of each other.

distinct(ion)
In trinitarian description, entities are *distinct* that can be thought of individually for the purpose of theological clarity. However, such entities need not be separate in reality. In the Trinity, Father, Son, and Spirit may and must be considered and described in *distinction* from one another. However, since together they constitute the one God, they can never be separated from each other.

| | |
|---|---|
| *economy of salvation* | The divine plan or design to overcome and reverse the effects of human sin and restore human beings to right relationship with God. |
| *economic Trinity* | The Father, Son, and Holy Spirit regarded from the standpoint of their work in the creation for human salvation. This idea is typically contrasted with the idea of the *immanent Trinity.* |
| *Enlightenment* | An eighteenth-century intellectual movement that encouraged confidence in reason, sense experience, and science, at the same time disparaging confidence in traditional religious authority as the standard for truth. |
| *essence* | Latin-derived term indicating the Greek *ousia*; that shared divine reality in which Father, Son, and Spirit are mutually and equally divine; that which distinguishes God as God. See also *being, substance, reality.* |
| *existence* | This English term is sometimes used to express the Greek term *hypostasis*, which indicates the Father, Son, and Holy Spirit in the distinction of their threeness. For example, the phrase "three distinct existences of the single divine reality." See also *person(a), subsistence.* |
| *filioque* | Greek phrase meaning "and from the Son." In the early Middle Ages, the Western, Latin-speaking church began to insert this phrase into the Nicene Creed in the Augustinian belief that the Holy Spirit eternally *proceeds* as a single principle from the Father and the Son together. See also *procession.* |
| *generat(ion/ed)* | The specific means by which the Son is said to eternally proceed from the Father; comparable to the term *begotten*. Cf. *procession.* |
| *heresy* | A theological teaching regarded in official church doctrine as misrepresenting the truth. |
| *homoousios* | "Of the identical substance." This term was adopted at the Council of Nicaea (325) in refutation of Arius, and thenceforth required in orthodox |

theology for proper description of the relationship of the Son to the Father.

*homoiousios*  "Of like (or similar) substance." Proposed but rejected as a compromise term to describe the relationship of the Son to the Father by those seeking rapprochement between the Arian and Alexandrian parties at the Council of Nicaea (325).

*hypostas(is/eis)*  The authoritative Greek term established by the Cappadocian theologians to refer to Father, Son, and Holy Spirit in their threeness, or distinction; a positive, concrete, particular, and distinct existence of a single shared reality. *Hypostaseis* is my English transliteration of the Greek plural used to refer to more than one *hypostasis*. See also *person(a), subsistence, existence.*

*immanent*  In theological discussion not concerned with the Trinity, *immanent* means near, close to, actively involved with, or dispersed in the world. Cf. *immanent Trinity.*

*immanent Trinity*  Father, Son, and Holy Spirit considered from the standpoint of God's internal relationships within God's own self.

*impassibility*  Imperviousness to feeling, suffering, passion, emotion, diversity, or change. Due to influence from Greek philosophy, Christian theology typically regarded *impassibility* as a divine attribute until recent studies began to point out the inconsistency of this idea with biblical depictions of God.

*koinonia*  Union with one another; mutual participation, commitment, concern, sharing, interconnectedness; open, unhindered interpersonal *communion.*

*modalism*  A misunderstanding of the unity of Father, Son, and Holy Spirit that compromises the genuine distinction of the three persons, by either (1) regarding them as only external modes, appearances, or manifestations of God, (2) associating the persons reductively with specific aspects of the divine work in the world (i.e., Father = Creator, Son = Redeemer, Spirit = Sustainer), or (3) viewing each person as a sequential expression of God in time.

**Modern**  In popular use this term is still frequently used to indicate anything contemporary or that has recently emerged in history. In theology and philosophy, however, the *Modern* period of history is usually regarded as beginning with the close of the Middle Ages in the sixteenth century and connected with the emergence of the European worldview emphasizing the power of human reason to address the deepest human questions, problems, and needs. The philosopher Descartes was a typical early proponent of a *Modern* worldview. Most philosophers and theologians now speak of the "Modern" period of history as having ended with World War I and the consequent loss of confidence in the powers of reason. Contemporary philosophical and theological trends are often described as "Post-Modern," since no clear alternative to Modernity has yet emerged.

**monotheism**  Belief in one God. For Christians convinced of the deity of Jesus Christ and the Holy Spirit, trinitarian faith guards and guarantees their *monotheism*, i.e. their continuity with and commitment to Yahweh, the one God of Israel. However, in Jewish and Muslim thought, *monotheism* is sometimes simplistically contrasted with trinitarianism as if the two were incompatible.

**necessary**  In theological use, something that is logically required in order to avoid self-contradiction.

**orthodox**  (1) Deriving from the Greek *doxa*, or "glory," the term has come to mean both "right praise" and, primarily, "right belief." (2) Later, belief or teaching that accords with the church's authoritative interpretations of scripture. (3) When capitalized, the term refers to the tradition of Christian faith associated originally with the Eastern half of the Roman Empire and defined by its use of the Greek language, a sphere that grew to encompass a variety of churches formed under Byzantine influence, including those of Syrian, Russian, and Slavic language and culture. E.g. "Eastern Orthodox" Christianity.

*ousia*    The definitive Greek term referring to the single shared divine reality that constitutes the divine oneness and distinguishes God as God. See also *being, essence, substance.*

*patriarchy*    Popularly understood, a system of social organization in which women are pervasively and oppressively subordinated (consciously or unconsciously) to fathers and men.

*perichoresis*    A term used to refer to the shared divine life of Father, Son, and Holy Spirit in their inexhaustible intercommunion, mutual inexistence, and mutual indwelling. Father, Son, and Holy Spirit dwell in one another and have their being in one another. Each inhabits the others. They are coterminous and coextensive. In each, the others are completely and wholly present. This term is of Greek derivation.

*person(a)*    (1) In trinitarian discourse, *person* (Latin: *persona*) is the term proposed by Tertullian and retained throughout the history of Western theology for referring to the Father, Son, and Holy Spirit in their distinction from each other. (2) More broadly, the idea of *person* as the distinct, particular existence of a being understood in its mutual interrelationships with other *persons* is a unique contribution of Christian thought to contemporary understandings of human identity. See also *hypostas(is/eis), subsistence, existence.*

*procession*    The eternal coming forth or origination of the Son and the Spirit from the Father within the internal life of the Trinity. The Son proceeds by being eternally *begotten* or born or *generated* from the Father. The Spirit proceeds by being eternally breathed forth (*spirated*) from the Father (or in the Western tradition, from the Father and the Son together as a single principle). See also *generation, spiration.*

reality

In this book, the term *reality* is often used to refer to the one divine *ousia*, being, essence, or substance that constitutes the divine oneness in traditional trinitarian theology. Thus, the Trinity may be described as three existences (Father, Son, and Holy Spirit) of the single divine *reality*. See also *being, essence, substance.*

redemption

"To redeem" is literally to buy back. In Christian theology, Jesus Christ accomplished human *redemption* by buying back fallen humanity for God at the cost of his own life, sacrificed on the cross. More broadly, *redemption* is often used as a near synonym for salvation.

revelation

The area of Christian theology concerned with how God has made the divine nature known to human beings.

separate

In trinitarian discussion, the word *separate* is not used to describe the mutual relationships between the Father, Son, and Holy Spirit. The three are *distinct*, since they can be separately considered in thought, but never separate, being one God.

spiration

The term used to refer to the mode of eternal procession of the Holy Spirit. It indicates the process of being "breathed forth," and is based on the Hebrew and Greek association of "Spirit" with "breath." See also *procession, begotten, generation.*

subordina-tionism

A misunderstanding of the unity of Father, Son, and Spirit that regards the Son and the Spirit as somehow less than fully divine, thus subordinating them to the Father.

substance

That shared divine reality in which Father, Son, and Spirit are mutually and equally divine. That which distinguishes God as God. See also *essence, being, ousia.*

subsistence

Common English translation of the Greek word *hypostasis*, the term used to refer to Father, Son, and

Holy Spirit in their distinction from each other. See also *hypostas(is/eis), person(a), existence.*

*Theism*

Broad, unspecified philosophical acknowledgment that one God is creator of the universe and is clearly distinct from and transcendent above that which is created.

*transcendence*

God's exaltedness above and beyond created reality; divine unknowability; God's utter unlikeness or perceived distance from the created world.

*tritheism*

Belief in three Gods. On one level, the doctrine of the Trinity is the Christian attempt—in light of the deity of the Son and the Spirit—to avoid tritheism and remain faithful to the declaration of Deut. 6:4: "Hear, O Israel, Yahweh our God is one."